SEARCH FOR A FATHER

SEARCH FOR A FATHER

The Amazing True Story of One Woman's
Search for Her Father

Amanda Lord
with Simon Lord

Authentic

MILTON KEYNES ● COLORADO SPRINGS ● HYDERABAD

Dedicated to the loving memory of Jenny Lord and Pam Curtis. Jenny will always be remembered for her strength – and the faith she shared with many. Pam will be remembered as a single mum who did the best with what she had, for her five children.

There are times I remember the conversations I had with Mum as an ungrateful teenager. I would love to have a conversation with her now as a 34-year-old woman who has grown through a remarkable journey.

But that will have to wait for another, brighter day.

Contents

Acknowledgements

Thanks to the following people:

My husband Tim, for standing by me and when I ran out of faith, for reminding me of the dream. My children – Danielle, Ethan and Joseph – thank you for your love, patience and understanding, for your prayers and belief in me. I am so proud of you all.

Special thanks to Amanda Hills for your faithful friendship and your obedience to God when he asked you to stand at the sidelines cheering me on through the tears and the joy. Pip and Paul Smith, and Jo Thatcher for your friendship. Thank you for believing in me, standing by me and joining us at the sideline of my race to meet my father.

To the youth group at ACC for your love and support, for the months of prayer, pictures and prophecy, the encouragement and for making me feel part of the family. Keep running and never give up your dreams.

To Christine Beales, for your faith that moves mountains, for your daily prayers and for your support in

Cyprus. You're a blessing to many. John Beales, for being my stand-in father, especially on my wedding day! Anna and Martin, for joining the journey, cheering me on and your prayers. Thank God for the dream he gave Anna, to encourage me, to believe with me.

To Arun Community Church: God sets the lonely in families and I am so thrilled he put me here! Thanks to all who encouraged and believed. Dave Cottrell for giving me the spiritual milk in the early days and for the freedom to dance! Becca for believing in Tim and me to work with the youth at ACC. Leigh Hills, for the tea!

To Tony Patoto, for catching the breeze and for your help. To JB (Jonathan Brown), for picking up the pace and carrying on. Thanks to Simon and Gemma, for being a part of the vision and believing, and for having the faith to start a book that did not even have an end.

To Sheila Jacobs and Clive Price, thanks for all your editorial work on the book.

To Andy – thanks for being a great family friend and a faithful father to your daughter.

To Jesus my Lord and Saviour, my Father God and the Holy Spirit. This story will be to your glory. Thank you.

Amanda Lord
March 2006

Forewords

Before Delirious? became Delirious? we used to lead an event called 'Cutting Edge' which began in 1992. It was a monthly gathering where anyone from the local churches in West Sussex could come and sing modern hymns to God. In fact, we did a whole lot more than that, we sang till our lungs almost burst, danced with abandoned passion, prayed to be more like our Creator and promised we would make a difference in the time we are alive. Most months, in the half-light of the school sports hall, I would be drawn to the face of a young lady whose one purpose in life was to find and follow Jesus. I remember her crying, laughing, dancing, healing, shouting and living like there was no tomorrow, as we saw her grow and become strong in her friendship with her heavenly Father.

It's only now that I have the pleasure of being friends with this young lady, all these years later, that I understand in part what was happening on those evenings and what courage it took Amanda to just be there.

I've read and heard of many 'heroes' of the faith and all of them possess two great qualities – 'faith' and 'courage'. In reading this book you will see that Amanda has extraordinary amounts of both to have pulled herself out of the past and into today. The search for her earthly father is not some Hollywood tale but like climbing up the north face of a mountain with an ice-cold blizzard in your face trying to stop you from feeling the sunshine at the top. This girl has tenacity with a capital T and understands grace with a capital G.

Read this book and you will find another 'hero', as I have done.

Martin Smith

There are so many ways to catch a glimpse of the magnificence of our God – gazing at the heavens, hearing the sounds of inspired music, that first glimpse of your newborn baby – but there is nothing quite as wonderful as the glory of a changed life; a life that was so very broken, and only through the indescribable love of Christ, is made whole *and* new. This is the wonder of the power of the cross, and its ability to change us from the inside out.

I pray that Amanda's compelling story about the tragedy of a life filled with the heartache of unrequited love, and the search for love that will not abuse or neglect, will inspire you to live a life worth living; a life that understands its value and worth; and that the power of this revelation will lead thousands of young women on this journey out of darkness, and into the glorious light of the love of God.

Thank you, Amanda, for not only deciding to stand and win, but for sharing the at times horrific, yet eventually victorious story of your life thus far. We stand alongside you, completely confident that all of your greatest days still lie in front of you.

With much love and respect

Darlene Zschech

Part I

Lost Horizons

1

Family Misfortunes

We grew up with the essentials and nothing more. That was reflected in the very basic home furnishings. Mum owned an old PVC armchair from which we were regularly dismissed. She did not like to be disturbed while engrossed in her literary worlds of James Herbert and Stephen King.

In the kitchen, the chip pan remained in a state of greasy overuse. Bread, cheese and cake would be left on the table for our tea. We couldn't rummage through the cupboards for interesting snacks and treats – our needs were catered for on a day-to-day basis. There was nothing luxurious or frivolous in the Curtis household.

I was born in 1972 in a small town near Eastbourne in the south of England. My mum's name was Pam Curtis and I was her fifth child, the youngest of five girls. I was the baby of the family, two years younger than my fourth sister Beverley and thirteen years younger than my eldest sister, Lynn.

Along with my sisters Carol and Marissa, we all had different fathers. Lynn's was a Greek Cypriot, Marissa's was Italian and Carol's was English. Bev's father was brought up in London, although he originated from

Barbados, and my father was also a Greek Cypriot. Sadly, despite the fact that there were five different men of mixed nationalities involved in creating my family, not one of them stayed to be a loving parent. To compensate, Mum became defiantly single-minded when it came to our upbringing.

Pam Curtis was a tall, slim woman with curly brown hair and glasses. She was attractive, but not trendy. I often looked at other children's mothers wishing that my mum could have been as fashionable as theirs.

Mum was fiercely independent. She worked hard at the local hospital for mental health patients, and she was proud of never having 'sponged off the social'. She was a heavy smoker. The house was thick with smoke and the ashtrays crammed with cigarette stubs. We were not an affluent family, but despite having very little spare cash, Mum always had a ready supply of cigarettes.

The three-bedroom terraced house left little space between us, which inevitably led to a lot of tension. Mum was always at work, so we sisters had to fend for ourselves. We created our own system of law and order. Even as a toddler, I developed a profound sense of being treated as something without value, observing the family's affairs from my increasingly dislocated world.

When I was three, Lynn left home to live with my nan. There was not enough room in the house for all six of us. As the eldest, she was often responsible for looking after her baby siblings. As the two youngest, Bev and I fought and played together on the communal green outside the house. All that separated Mum's territory from this grassy expanse was a tiny front garden and a narrow path, linking the road to the rabbit warren of the housing estate.

Ten houses, in total, surrounded the neighbourhood green. In the summer months, all the neighbours met together on the turf. The mothers lay on their makeshift sunbeds of towels and blankets, drinking tea and smoking John Player Special cigarettes. They waddled, chatting, from garden to garden, like geese. Their sunburnt kids wrestled and played in the thick summer heat. Some of the families kept to themselves, but the majority knew everyone – and everyone's business. It was an intimate community which thrived on gossip and lived under the stigma of its council estate reputation. Even so, it was always desirable to be a cut above the neighbours. The same snobbery was readily applied to even less attractive parts of the estate than ours.

As I grew older, Mum would send me out onto the green to play and I would immediately disappear elsewhere. I played with Roy and Alan, the two boys next door. We laughed one minute and fought the next. Occasionally, fistfuls of coal were thrown like hand grenades over the garden fence. One sunny day, Mum was out and Marissa had assumed control. The boys hurled their washing line pole into our garden and it hit me. Marissa saw them from the kitchen window and exerted her fiery authority. If Marissa wasn't arguing with Mum, she was fighting with Carol, and she had beaten Bev up on more than a few occasions. She was a rebel and became a skinhead to prove it. So it was well within her temperament to throw the pole back like a javelin. She scored a direct hit on one of the boys and their dad got involved.

Arguments quickly escalated in a neighbourhood that could be volatile. But even through the conflict there was room for close and caring friendships. Mum was often next door, borrowing the life essentials – milk and cigarettes.

Mum's reputation was of somebody you did not mess around with. If any of the local women had problems with Bev or Marissa, few would make it an issue. With five children, Mum had to fulfil the role of both parents in her authority and protection. I remember one instance when she was ironing the family clothes. A lady from the estate stuck her head through the living room window to complain about Carol. Mum ripped the iron from the wall and charged towards the unwelcome neighbour, screaming and swearing. Her territory and reputation were never compromised. She was a fearsome opponent who did not suffer fools gladly. I asked her once if she thought I was a fool. Her answer was, 'Yes.'

Over the years, I had watched with interest as my sisters progressed through school. By the time I was ready to begin primary school, Carol and Marissa were already in their senior school years. I tried to keep up with the schoolwork. I remember not being able to spell my own name; I struggled to keep up with the lessons. My innocent mistakes, once seen as charming and naïve, became humiliating when people laughed at me long after infancy. It was the condemnation and shame that lingered. As a result I often avoided class by sitting in the sick room. Here I was known as 'the poor girl who never had a temperature'. I was flattered that people at least cared enough to notice me. At home I never received any affection from Mum.

Eventually, I was assigned to the remedial group. Despite being separated from my friends and branded 'remedial', I liked my new class. We took advantage of being placed in an environment where nothing was expected from us. With no one to catch up with and nothing to achieve, we fell behind even further. People thought we were stupid, and so it was easier to play along than to try and prove otherwise.

Academically I had no aspirations. Mum had issued all the family with labels and she often reminded us of our standing in life. Lynn was beautiful. She was studying catering at college, and we were all aware of how successful she would become. Carol was the clever one who carried a banner of perfection. This was often waved over us as proof of our own shortcomings. She became my second mum and I was very close to her, but there was a huge pressure on Carol to live up to her image of perfection.

Marissa suffered a lot of rejection for not being like Carol. She was fiery like Mum, but Marissa's passion was considered selfish and rebellious. I once returned home from school to find children's bodies strewn over the living room floor. I could hear Marissa, upstairs, throwing up in a bucket. Thinking everybody was ill on account of the groaning, I phoned Mum, who arrived home to a house full of drunken children. Marissa was always fighting the world; she once threatened Carol with a hot poker, and ran away from home to join the local fair. Under Marissa's guidance I learned how to smoke, skive off school and steal Mum's money and cigarettes. I then shared my new-found skills and knowledge with my friends at primary school.

Bev had a violent temper, but she was Mum's favourite. When she was not locked in combat with the neighbourhood kids, she was either fighting at school or beating me up at home. Our fights were horrendous. She would pull me upstairs by the hair and smack my head against furniture. It was real violence with Bev, black eyes and bruises, but it was her way of trying to cope with a world that bullied her on account of her dark skin. After another boring day, I would sprint across the nearby field to see who was involved in any after-school brawls. It was often Bev, entangled with a couple of girls or boys because they had called her offensive names. Even as a skinny little girl, I used to pull people away as I tried passionately to protect my sister. I was bullied in primary school for being remedial and for not wearing the nicest clothes, but even adults threw racist insults at Bev. She was neither black nor white, with no real place to belong. The bullying made Bev very fearful and she rarely left the house after school.

My label was 'the thick one of the family'. Carol once asked us all what we wanted to do when we grew up. I said that I wanted to be a home help because I liked to clean, but Carol replied that I should be more ambitious. Mum defended my lack of ambition by saying that I was simply being realistic. It was the label pinned on me by my family and teachers, and it became woven into the very fabric of my self-belief.

In my last year at primary school, a new teacher joined who wanted to teach dance. I soon discovered that I had a talent for dancing, and I remember my teacher saying in exasperated relief, 'Thank God we've found something you're good at.' The compliment was double-edged. On the one hand it encouraged me to dance, but it also reinforced that I could not do anything else.

In a school production of *Peter and the Wolf*, I played the part of a songbird which was in every scene. The teachers thought I was amazing and I even performed a dance solo to end the evening. A local reporter photographed the event. The headmaster praised my dancing to Mum, suggesting that she found me some dance lessons. I was a quick learner, picking up the moves and routines from observation alone, but unfortunately we could not afford the proper tuition. By the time I was at senior school I was dancing among girls who had received lessons since they were infants. My confidence was crushed as once again I fell short of the expected standard. I knew that, had I been able to have such lessons, I could have excelled in the one thing that gave me hope to believe I was anything other than simply 'thick'.

During these early years, squabbling and fighting in the sibling ranks beneath Mum, I learned a lesson that made an indelible mark on my development. When I was about four years old I very innocently questioned Mum about my body. From her throne-like armchair and armed with her royal cup of tea and cigarettes, Mum decided to teach me – and my sister, Bev – about the facts of life. Mum explained that while sex was something she enjoyed, she never wanted a lasting relationship with a man. She was too independent. There was no way on earth that a man would tell her how to live her life. She told us how she slept with married men because there were no strings attached. And she neither loved nor kissed a man. Sex was sex, nothing more and nothing less. Mum was very proud of not being the 'sort of silly woman' who would have an affair, only to then expect the man to leave his wife for her. In fact, if the men she slept with showed any signs of deeper affection, she would be quick to get rid of them.

That was her outlook, tainted by a twisted pride in never having broken up a marriage. Mum's practice was to use men for sex. Her teaching was that if men were to be used in this way, then as women we should not think of ourselves as any different. I often wonder whether my mum's attitude was formed because she never knew her own father.

Sometimes people think of abuse as being only physical. Society is stained with accounts of abusers and their victims caught in a cycle of physical pain, fear and guilt. But I believe that my abuse began when Mum spoke her parental teaching over my young mind. Mum stood at the helm of the Curtis family. She was the authority and standard that my sisters and I measured our lives against. She was our role model. But her brutal attitude towards something so intimate cut a deep incision in my perception of the world. The consequences would later prove to be devastating.

2

Father Figures

Occasionally Mum entertained a visitor or two. I would sometimes arrive home from school, dishevelled and bored, to find Mum talking with strangers. I remember one foreign man in particular. He and Mum engaged in their grown-up talk, while I floated around them like a ghost. I was only ever spoken to while being formally addressed by an adult. I was never picked up or played with. I had to amuse myself in my invisible little five-year-old world.

The conversation revolved around my eldest sister Lynn, and it transpired that Mum's guest was in fact Lynn's father, Stelios. This was odd; I was intrigued. *So people have dads then*, I thought.

We sat on the sofa with Greek Stelios in the middle. His male presence inspired me to ask Mum a question.

'Who's my dad, then? If this is Lynn's dad, who's *my* dad?'

I tried to get Mum's attention, repeating the question over and over. In the end, I asked the man, 'Are *you* my dad?'

Eventually, Mum snapped, 'I'm not telling you who your dad is.'

I pleaded with her. '*Why* won't you tell me?' A lump came to my throat. 'Is it because he doesn't want to know me?'

Then the brutal truth. 'He doesn't even know you exist.'

'Mum, *please* tell him about me.'

'No.'

I felt close to tears. 'Is it because he wouldn't *want* to know me?'

'It's the opposite,' said Mum, shortly. 'He *would* want to know. He was married at the time and you know me, I am not willing to wreck a marriage.'

My protest continued until Mum told me that my father's name was Terry. Stelios had introduced them at a house-warming party, and apparently Terry had been the best looking man in the room – although this hardly made me feel any better. The day after the party, one of Mum's friends from the green asked how she had 'got on with that man', only to find him walking down the stairs.

Nine months later, I was born.

I pleaded with Mum one last time to tell my dad about me, but Stelios told me to respect Mum's wishes and leave it alone. I was wounded, thinking that Mum's protection of a secret affair was more important than my desire to know about my father. Any chance of a relationship with him had been severed.

Mum and I didn't have a great relationship in terms of communication. Not once did she tell me that she loved me, and so I believed that she didn't. But from that day, I cut myself off from her emotionally. She became a distant figure in my life.

Lynn's father, Stelios, had gone out with Mum for about two years until Mum discovered she was pregnant with his child. Mum viewed the Greek Cypriot culture with cold suspicion, because most of the Cypriot men she had met kept mistresses. She refused to stay with Stelios and agreed not to ask for any money, but he made fleeting visits every six months or so. He eventually moved to Australia and Lynn never saw her father again.

Another visitor was Stelios's brother, Paul.

I remember being at home one day because I was sick with the mumps. I was too contagious to attend school and so I lay outside recovering in the sun. While I sunbathed with Carol, Paul arrived and gave us each some money. Paul owned a Greek restaurant, so it was not surprising to see him carrying loads of cash. It always came straight from the pocket, from a roll of worn notes sealed with a simple elastic band. This always impressed me, and it was not long before I had spent these casual gifts on sweets and ice cream.

Carol once threw him out of Mum's house because he tried to molest her. She may have been the perfect one of the family, but she was still tarred with the same brush as Mum. In Paul's eyes, if Pam was up for it, then so were her older daughters. During his visits, he and Mum would have lengthy debates on the subservient role of women. I imagined his wife to be little more than an overworked and under-appreciated house slave.

Carol's father was initially unaware of her existence. Mum surprised him during a phone call, saying that his daughter was home from school. She invited him to come and meet Carol for the first time, which he did, only to disappear again.

I never heard Marissa mention her father; all I knew was that he was Italian.

Bev's father used to spend time with her when she was a baby. He was a social worker, and he had about twelve children as a result of sowing his seed across the world. We occasionally visited him and his wife in London, but ultimately these occasions only served to hurt Bev. She would scream and cry, expressing her hatred towards the family because she wanted to live with her father. However, he never sent her birthday cards or presents. He was juggling so many stray children that contact was strictly on his terms.

Another man who walked in and out of my life was my uncle. His sporadic visits always generated a lot of excitement. In actual fact, he was not my uncle at all; he was my mum's uncle. But he didn't have any children, so he and his wife would make an incredible fuss of us, treating us to sweets and presents. He was fun to be with and we trusted him. Even Mum thought highly of him. I latched on to him because he always responded positively to my needs. There was no other father figure in my life and I don't remember a man ever living with us in the house. Mum 'entertained' her male guests, but never had boyfriends. Any relationships she had took place in the secrecy of night, while we were all fast asleep.

When I was seven, and still at primary school, my uncle and auntie were asked to baby-sit for me at their house. Auntie had an appointment at the hairdressers, and so I joined them for the ride as Uncle dropped her off and drove back home again. In his wife's absence, he showed me some family photographs hanging on the wall, pictures that I had already seen a hundred times before. Not being tall enough to see them properly, he picked me up, but as he did, he surreptitiously placed his hand between my legs.

As my attention was diverted to the wall of photographs, he rubbed his hand against me while holding me firmly in place. I immediately froze inside. It was a terrible feeling. I was completely trapped and I knew that if I had challenged him he would have denied everything. After all we were simply looking at photographs, but they had become a masquerade for something far more sinister.

Although it went no further than that one sleazy, lingering moment, I could not speak to him for the duration of the day. We drove out again to pick Auntie up from the hairdressers. Although I wasn't a confident child, I was quite loud and open with people. Auntie noticed my silence on this occasion and asked me whether I was feeling OK. I don't know what suspicions inspired her next question, but she turned sharply to my uncle and asked, 'What have you done?'

'Nothing!' he replied, brusquely.

While he drove us home, I sat in the back seat, violated, ashamed and afraid. The safety and trust of our relationship had been shattered by my uncle's brief moment of perverted pleasure.

One day the police called at our house, and informed Mum that my uncle had died. He worked as a milkman and while out on his round, he had fallen over and collapsed – he'd had a heart attack. I was shocked but also very confused and angry about his behaviour towards me. Now I'd never be able to ask him why he did what he did to me. But there was a deep sadness too. I felt very sorry for my auntie, but thankfully Mum was a great support to her. The extended family had regarded Mum with a degree of social shame for having five children by five different fathers. But she was also the one person they all turned to in a crisis. I did not turn to Mum about my own crisis with Uncle, even though I'd hated him at the time. I struggled with the need to share what he had done, but in the end I chose not to. It was enough that he was dead.

Even as early on as primary school, I never expected to be loved; I certainly didn't expect to be loved by Mum. Since she wouldn't tell my father about me, it was as if our relationship had been emotionally cut off at the root. We had nowhere to grow as mother and daughter, and so I began to develop my own survivalist approach to life. Other children would run home from school to see their parents, but I deliberately made it a long and arduous trek. In my first years of school, I would often return to friends' houses instead of my own. It never occurred to me that Mum would be worried; it was ingrained in me that she didn't care.

I bound myself to a girl called Lisa. When Lisa returned home from school, she was given her ten-month-old baby sister and a banana. Her parents would then kick her out of the house with orders not to return until later. While Mum was at work, Lisa practically lived at my house and she would scream whenever Bev beat me up. Otherwise we would hang around the streets until dark, carrying her baby sister like a parcel with no destination. I felt sorry for Lisa. Her mother was divorced and living with a partner, and because she was Roman Catholic, the Church had excommunicated her. Even in my earliest years, I thought religion stank, yet I also somehow knew that this cold treatment was not from God. Surely God, if he existed at all, was against making people's lives even more miserable? Sometimes, when I wasn't hanging around with Lisa, I played with a couple of African girls who had been fostered by an elderly couple from the estate. They were loved and spoiled by their foster parents and were always dressed in the latest gear. We used to hold our own private dancing competitions in Mum's front room. However, Mum didn't like the company I was keeping. She saw my delayed homecomings from school as defiant, and her solution was to blame my friends. I was therefore banned from seeing them. This ultimately made matters worse, because I then had to see my friends behind Mum's back, risking further punishment.

The route I took home from school twisted and turned through the estate. I was walking home one day with a friend, and we passed the tiny bungalow of an old woman in a wheelchair. She called to us, asking whether we would like to take her dogs for a walk, offering to pay us with money or chocolate. Mum didn't like animals and so pets had been banned from our house. I jumped at the invitation to spend some time with this lady's wonderfully scruffy dogs. After a few weeks of giving them some exercise, the old lady, Mary, began to invite us in. She gave my sister and me cigarettes for walking the dogs, and we soon became friends.

The bungalow was tiny. The kitchen, bathroom and bedroom were all very compact, but it had a more spacious lounge. There were no carpets because of Mary's wheelchair, and the entire house was smothered in dog hair, which stank. There was a huge table in the lounge, laden with chocolate bars and hundreds of cigarettes. Mary gave me free rein to take what I pleased. Needless to say, this became a regular pitstop between school and home. The word quickly spread about this private paradise. Soon, lots of young girls ate chocolate, watched television and smoked in Mary's lounge.

Mary needed our help with her household chores, especially the washing up, which she found difficult to do from her wheelchair. She became our new mum, constantly praising and saying how lovely my sister Bev and I were. On one occasion, her house was full of stray schoolgirls and Mary began to cry. Despite being surrounded by young and upset faces, there was nothing we could do or say to stop her tears. She eventually told us that her husband sexually abused her. He was an out-patient at the local mental hospital where Mum worked. Through her tears, Mary told us in graphic detail of her husband's cruelty, sharing with her young fans the grue-some illustrations of her sex life. Not that I understood. I thought, *Poor lady*, because I didn't like to see her so upset.

When her husband was home, he would say that he was the daddy we never had, inviting us to sit on his lap to be cuddled. I wasn't fond of him at all, but Mary would tell me how much he liked me. When Mum found out, she told us not to spend time in the house if Mary's hus-band was present. She didn't mind us walking the dogs, but she even warned us about Mary too, claiming that the elderly couple were as devious as each other.

'I've heard of these two before,' said Mum, 'and they've got a reputation. Don't be fooled by the woman – she's just as bad as him. You have to promise never to go there when he's around.'

Of course, Mum's warnings only fuelled my need to continue visiting these surrogate parents. At Mary's house my chocolate-scoffing, cigarette-smoking indul-gences were greatly encouraged. The old woman had won my affections, and I cared about her.

I remember being at the bungalow alone. Mary left the lounge to do the washing up, which was unusual. Her husband invited me to sit on his lap because he wanted to be my daddy. He slid his hand up my skirt, but I stopped him before he managed to touch me. Once again I froze inside, but this time I was quick to escape, and I departed with a cold goodbye to Mary. I walked home in silence, never to return.

We received another visit from the police, but this time they wanted to talk to Bev and me. Mum invited them in, and the policewoman asked openly whether Mary or her husband had ever sexually abused us. Bev said that she had found him a bit creepy, and I told them exactly what had happened to me. The policewoman said I was very brave, but I didn't feel brave. I was simply delivering direct answers to direct questions. It was easy to express such a blasé attitude, because I was becoming so emotionally distant to the world.

We were told that Mary's husband had dragged a local girl into a brick cubicle, which functioned as a communal washing line area, where he had raped her. It appeared that Mum's warnings of them being as evil as each other had been justified. Wheelchair-bound Mary had enticed local girls into the house, and her husband had abused them whenever the opportunity arose.

So much for surrogate parents!

3

Dark Room

She was in her bedroom, on her bed, with a man lying on top of her. Not knowing where to look, I was distracted by his cowboy boots, which was all he was wearing.

Neither of them had seen me, and so I silently left the room in a state of shock. When Bev arrived home, I immediately told her that Mum was upstairs with a stranger. Our inquisitive squeals prompted Mum's swift appearance from the bedroom. She quickly diverted us with money, sending us out to the shops.

When we returned, the man in the cowboy boots, now fully clothed, had relocated to the sofa.

'Oh, look who's come to visit!' said Mum, with a touch of melodrama. Her performance continued as one of her friends from the green called round.

'He was a bit drunk, and so I had to sober him up,' Mum continued, signalling upstairs with her eyes. I knew what she was doing. And I wanted her to know that I knew.

'I walked in on you earlier, so don't you *dare* pretend that I don't know what you're on about,' I told her. 'I know *exactly* what you're talking about.'

Mum could not hide her embarrassment, or her disappointment, that I had seen her with the cowboy. But I had a point to make. I was growing up, and I was no longer the little fool that she took me for.

Senior school was my chance to move away from the chequered pattern of my short life. I didn't want to be bullied any more for being remedial, for not having nice things, and so I made an extra effort in my appearance. I wanted to present myself as somebody attractive and appealing.

On my first day I was determined to make the right impression. Unfortunately, my neighbour Roy, who was in my new class, told everybody that I hung around with gypsies. At the time, there was a gypsy family living across the green. Most families stayed forever, but this particular house hosted a variety of people who moved in and out. I played with their children along with everyone else's. And so despite my initial attempt at reinvention, I was now known as 'gypsy' because I was friendly with them. It became my new label, the first of many.

The father of one of my classmates used to work with Mum at the hospital, and his daughter and I became friends. But her parents warned her away from me, as apparently I had a potential evil influence, based on Mum's reputation. Mum was hardly infamous, but the social scandal of her sleeping with so many men was evident in her daughters' appearances. Unfortunately Bev stood out the most, and I was frequently asked, 'How can you two be sisters? Is she adopted?' Despite any explanations I could think of, I was bullied simply for being Bev's sister. Bev retaliated with everything she had, whereas I would scream and run away to cry.

These secondary school years became another period of dread, and so I followed Marissa's example and played truant. It was easier for me to cut school out of the picture than to endure the bullying and embarrassment. Marissa taught me that I could get away with it. Mum's house became the local truancy hotspot. If the house wasn't available, then smoking in the stink of the town centre toilets was still preferable to being bored and bullied in class. My name developed from 'thick', to 'gypsy' to 'faggy', because of the lingering smell of stale cigarettes.

Smoking cigarettes became an early addiction for me. Mum knew about it because she had caught me smoking in the toilet, and her cigarettes went missing quicker than she could replace them. She decided to take charge, giving Bev and me a cigarette each. We were told not to smoke on the way home from school in case we were seen, but it was now official that we could smoke around the house. Mum confined smoking to her sphere of control, and her prescribed remedy was cause for celebration. At thirteen I was already smoking dope, and I began to plan my time around these seductive pursuits.

When I was in my young teens, the summer holidays were great. Every summer, foreign students, most of them French, invaded the small town where I lived, and Eastbourne. As a way of making some extra cash, Mum and our neighbour let students lodge in their homes. The French boys paid me compliments that I never received from my English peers. None of the boys at school would go out with me. My name had been smeared by years of insults and bullying, and so my friends and I would meet our French boyfriends in the park.

I shared my summer flirtations with my new friend, Michelle. She was a few years older than me, and enjoyed a reputation of being a 'woman of the world'. I was in awe of her streetwise confidence, but I was also afraid of her as she regularly bullied me.

This particular summer was fading, and the students were disappearing back to their homes across the Channel. Michelle and I were over at her parents' house. I liked her hairstyle and she had offered to cut my hair in the same fashion. After sitting in her house for five minutes we were joined by two of Michelle's brothers. They were both older than me, and although I recognised them from around town, I didn't know either of them. They mysteriously disappeared upstairs with their sister, while I was left sitting downstairs waiting to be transformed.

They were gone for a while and I began to wonder why. Suddenly Michelle summoned me upstairs, and as I reached the top, she swiftly passed me on her way back down. Before I had time to think, her brothers grabbed me and bundled me into their parents' bedroom. In a moment of violence I was thrown onto the double bed. One of the boys held me down, while the other tore off my clothes. Throughout the attack I pushed, struggled and screamed, but an unyielding hand was clamped over my mouth to stifle any further protest. One of the attackers looked directly into my eyes. I met his wide-eyed, adrenaline-fuelled stare with my own expression of complete terror.

'Stop it!' I heard. 'She's not up for it like Michelle said!'

He was right, I wasn't up for it, not in any way imaginable. But any momentary realisation of that fact didn't make the slightest difference; it was not enough to stop both of Michelle's brothers from raping me.

When they had finished, we all returned downstairs. The two boys complained to their sister about how I had not been as willing as she had led them to believe.

Michelle, who was offended by my lack of co-operation, looked at me accusingly.

'What's the matter?' she snapped. 'Aren't my brothers good enough for you?'

I was numb. I couldn't speak, and so I sat down . . . and let her cut my hair.

On the way home I thought about what I should do. Should I tell the police? Should I tell Mum? Michelle's toxic words haunted me. I decided to stay silent, telling myself that none of it really mattered. After all, Mum had once said, 'Sex is sex, nothing more and nothing less.' Tomorrow was another day, and so I returned home to see Mum. But, although I was able to block the incident from my mind, there was nothing I could do to stop the poison from infecting my heart.

I was incapable of reflecting on how these incidents were affecting my life. Mum had set my lot before me, saying that men were there to be used and therefore so was I. It was like a snowflake that would one day become an avalanche. As the abuse became acceptable, I allowed the snow to settle. But in my continued silence the shifting snow, full of menace, would begin to move. If I had been taught value instead of insignificance, I would not have blamed myself in the light of Michelle's words.

I began to sit in my bedroom, making the room as dark as I possibly could. Only then could I look at myself in the mirror. I hated the weak and pathetic reflection that cried back at me. I had always been told that I was stupid and ugly.

Michelle's words would echo round my brain. What *was* the matter with me?

I continued to use dope, smoking my way through different groups of friends. However, when I was out with my old friends, the African girls, I found myself dancing and enjoying the nightclub scene. The three of us loved to dance and, being immune to my vices, they would often stop me from smoking by snatching my cigarettes away.

The African girls were good for me. Life with them revolved around striving to be the best dancer in the local nightclubs. I used my skills to receive the male attention that I craved, and this gave me confidence. While I danced with men and enjoyed the spotlight, I made a lot of new friends. Unfortunately, nightclubbing had its seedy side, and as usual I was ill-equipped to deal with it.

One night, I met a couple of men who were dressed in smart suits. I thought they looked fantastic. It was a Friday night and so we danced and flirted. I arranged to meet with one of them the following afternoon; he wore his suit again and carried an air of success and popularity. We made a further agreement to meet for a drink. When we met, he said he had to make a quick visit to his flat.

'Do you want to come with me?' he said. 'You could meet my sister.'

'OK,' I replied, thinking, *Why not? What can be the harm in that?*

In reality, his flat was a squalid bedsit and his sister made a hurried exit as soon as we arrived. I felt extremely vulnerable, and it soon became clear that meeting his sister wasn't really what this man had in mind for me. There was no violence in his advances, but I didn't seem to be able to say 'No', despite every part of me wanting to scream it in his face.

I could only respond to this pattern like a rabbit caught in headlights, too frozen in fear to move. I told myself that it would soon be over and then I could go.

He took what he wanted, I felt sick, and then made another defeated journey home. Mum was working nights, and my friend – one of the African girls – had come round to sleep over. I told her about my encounter and burst into tears. It was the first time that I had shared any of these experiences with anyone. It wasn't until I started to cry that I began to feel the weight of the abuse. But after speaking to my friend, I buried the incident in the back of my mind; locked it away in the fearful shadows of a dark room. It became another incident to ignore, but little did I know, the avalanche was gaining momentum.

4

Lonely World

'Mandy Curtis' was becoming a dirty name. My experiences with boys had begun before I moved out of home. Due to Mum's absence and my older sisters' interests, there had always been boys around the house. So I had grown up dreaming about having a boyfriend of my own.

At the age of fifteen, I served as a waitress at a local wedding. I met a boy who all the girls wanted to dance with. We shared a romantic slow dance together, and from that moment on, I convinced myself that I was in love. I asked him to go out with me at school, but he said no. We did eventually meet up, but it had to be in secret because he didn't want his friends to know about me.

Our secret relationship lasted for over a year. I slept with him and then hid whenever his mates came round. As a fifteen-year-old, sex was something that I was prepared to do if it meant keeping hold of a boyfriend. Mum had once boasted of how sex was the only way to make a man respond to her, but my experience of sex had left me either cold or terrified.

I eventually rejected my boyfriend – but only because I had met someone else. I was diving in and out of relationships with no real knowledge of what I was doing. In my heart, I knew that Mandy Curtis had become a bit of a slut.

When I was sixteen, I finally moved away from home. Mum had always said that she was sick of my company and could not wait for me to leave. I relished the thought of leaving Mum's house and the town where I'd been brought up. I didn't only want to leave home behind, I wanted to leave Mandy Curtis behind too. So from that moment on, I decided that I'd be Amanda.

My aim was to prove to myself and to the world that not only could I survive, but I could succeed. My time had come, my bags were packed and the taxi was waiting. As I turned at the doorstep to say goodbye to Mum, I noticed a tear in her eye.

'Mand, aren't you going to give us a hug?' said Mum. 'You're the baby of the family – and you're leaving home!'

'Oh sorry, Mum,' I responded, turning towards her.

'Take care of yourself, girl,' she said.

It struck me as bizarre that Mum could possibly be sad about my leaving. I never felt that she had much affection for me. I gave her a quick hug and walked away.

I moved to a place called Waldron and became a nanny, but I gained little satisfaction from this, and so I moved again, to Eastbourne. I stayed with my sister, Carol, who helped me find another post as a nanny, this time in Henfield. Again, the work was boring, but the job had its perks. It allowed me to pretend to be a part of a new family. Here I could fantasise about love, acceptance and stability. Before long, I met another boy and I plunged myself into a relationship with him.

We moved to a seaside town, Worthing, which had a reputation for being a big sleepy retirement home for the elderly. My new boyfriend had been training to become a social worker. He gave it up to follow his romantic dream in which we would be married and in love forever. But my own fantasies of romance had already faded, and the relationship became as dull as my job.

The honeymoon periods of my relationships were great for as long as I could step outside of myself and indulge in fantasy. However, when my true identity began to surface, I was faced with all the horrible emotions that I was trying to run away from. When I escaped from the town where I'd grown up, I'd taken a lot more than material possessions with me. The fantasy of being in love was exciting and addictive, but the hurting, damaged little girl inside always returned, dumping her insecure baggage at my door. I began to adopt a defensive posture; I was going to reject the world, before it had a chance to discover and reject what I so despised about myself. Usually I rejected men before they rejected me; sometimes it was the other way round. Anyway, I was always moving on to somebody new – new excitement, a new promise of hope. The dull relationship over, I was looking for someone else; I never sat on the shelf of rejection very long.

While working in the local pub, I noticed one particular customer who would arrive dressed in an immaculate suit. He looked great. Surprisingly, he would glance over and look at me.

He looks too good for me, I said to myself, *he would never really pay me any attention.*

This went on for a few weeks until he asked me to meet him at another pub. I was gobsmacked. I waited in that seedy pub for a long time before he arrived.

'I can't believe that you waited so long for me,' he said. 'No one has ever done that for me before.'

I was hooked. Chris had his own sad story. His father had sexually abused him, and he had spent months convalescing in bed after a recent car crash. During this time his wife had had an affair. They split up and he'd had to give up his house and his children.

I quickly became obsessed with this tragic man of the world. When we were together, he treated me as though I was the only woman he had ever loved. It was such a wonderful feeling.

Sometimes I would wait for days to meet with him. He could disappear for weeks, only to re-emerge from obscurity, suddenly appearing in the pub while I was working my bar shifts. Despite feeling the dull and sickening pain of rejection, we would see each other again and the cycle would continue. When Chris wasn't playing such games he was dealing drugs. I liked taking drugs, and so I was soon reacquainted with old habits.

I moved from the familiarity of smoking dope into the more stimulating family of speed, acid and cocaine. In this respect, life with Chris and his dealer friends was never dull. I started getting high every weekend and sometimes at work.

There was always an abundance of money and drugs in Chris's world. He kept stashes of money everywhere, hiding close to a thousand pounds under my mattress. One night in the pub, he was so high that he started frantically searching through his clothes and pockets. He continued his paranoid rant in the street, convinced that he had lost his precious drugs money. In a fit of rage, he punched his fist through the window of a high street bank. His hand was cut to ribbons. The police caught up with us at the local Accident and Emergency department. I was covered in blood from having wrapped some clothing around Chris's lacerated hand. Meanwhile Chris gibbered like a madman, flitting from rage to self-pity. The police arrested us and put us in a cell for the night. After this incident I didn't see Chris for about a month. He eventually faded and disappeared. In the wake of our destructive relationship, I came crashing back down to earth.

Drug dealer Chris had kept me on a short rope of emotional and drug dependence. But as that relationship ground to a halt, I became even more determined to win the affection and approval of the world.

Looking after myself by my own strength had become as difficult as facing up to my weaknesses. I coped with life by throwing myself into relationships, and coped with relationships by throwing away my life. Relationships became my be all and end all; I worshipped them. I was still working in the pub and it wasn't long before the next man strolled into my lonely world of ashtrays and stale beer.

His name was Andy. I remember talking to Andy and his mates, joking and laughing while I closed the bar for the night. It had been a quiet Monday evening, and they had waited to walk me home. I invited Andy round for a meal, but because he was shy he insisted on bringing a friend. A couple of days later they both turned up. A few drinks soon softened the edge of Andy's embarrassment, and so we ate and went out. And that's how my next relationship began.

Andy had the reputation of being a local lunatic, but I saw another side of him that was vulnerable and shy. It wasn't long before I discovered that he had just come out of prison, having served three years for GBH (grievous bodily harm). In fact he had been in and out of prison most of his life, since attending a boys' borstal at the age of thirteen. It appeared that Andy was seldom out of trouble. He liked possessing the freedom to pursue his other interests while I was tucked safely behind the bar; here his friends could keep a close eye on me.

His approach to our relationship was as unhealthy as mine; our combined insecurities were a recipe for disaster.

From the very beginning of our time together, Andy stamped his control all over me. He would point out that I looked ugly, complain that I had bad skin, and how if he looked liked me he wouldn't dare leave the house! When Andy was mean and uncaring, I didn't get angry; my lack of confidence was such that I just desperately wanted to prove I was worthy of his love. My already fragile self-esteem crumbled completely under this warped, twisted view of Mandy Curtis. I began to believe the lie that I really was ugly and stupid.

And yet, despite everything that was initially wrong about us being together, the relationship with Andy was exciting. The hard-man reputation carried by Andy and his entourage held a fascination for me. I was attracted to this dangerous image. People were terrified of him.

'Amanda, what are you doing?' asked one of the regulars. 'Do you know that he went to prison for slashing someone's throat? Don't mess with him!'

'But I can see a softer side to him,' I pleaded. 'He's not all bad.' Later, Andy cornered that customer in the toilets and threatened him.

I didn't listen to the warnings. I saw myself as capable of changing Andy for the better. His whole persona was a challenge. But I was determined to tame and domesticate this wild man. We had a fun time going out, getting stoned, taking pills and drinking. But according to Andy, I was merely a convenient alternative to staying at his mum's house.

He told me never to think that he could ever fall in love with me, because the only person he loved was his mum. It was like the stereotypical mother and son relationship seen in popular fiction. The son could lie, cheat and beat someone senseless – but his dear old mum wouldn't mind – as long as he remained loyal and tied to her apron strings!

Meanwhile, I was working long hours to pay my way. I had two jobs, working at a nursing home during the day and serving at the pub until midnight. This was a routine that I managed easily. But three months into my new relationship I found myself exhausted, sometimes too tired to get out of bed.

After missing a period, I went to a chemist's to buy a pregnancy test kit. The whole experience was like entering forbidden territory. I felt as if people were staring at me in the shop. I fled into the night and took the kit home. Hidden away in our small, narrow bathroom, I followed the cold and clinical instructions to the letter. The grim ritual seemed to take a long time. But it was only seconds later that the fateful blue line appeared.

I was pregnant.

Part of me was really excited about this change. It was a new journey. I was eighteen – and there was a baby growing inside me. It was an adventure. However, another part of me was overwhelmed and very frightened.

Accepting my condition was one thing – thinking about keeping the baby was another. There was no one around to help me with an answer. Being the youngest of five sisters, there had always been someone around to tell me what to do, whether I had wanted to hear it or not.

Now I was alone.

I remember physically collapsing under the pressure of having to make the decision by myself. I fell on my knees, sobbing. I had set out on a new journey to prove that I could do something with my life. Now here I was, stranded. I felt I had failed myself. Should I keep this baby? Or should I be free? It was the hardest decision. I still didn't know my father – but I could know this baby if I wanted to. And no one could take that away from me.

5

Baby Danielle

I threw myself into being pregnant. It was all that I was going to concentrate on. So I stopped working at both the nursing home and the pub. I claimed benefits, receiving £36 a week – with no idea of how to budget such a meagre amount of cash.

From earning lots to claiming little meant that I had to change my lifestyle. I found a room in a shared house, and moved in with two girls. This was difficult, as I was seen as a suspicious addition to their household – single, pregnant, and out to take whatever I could. We shared the house but nothing else. When the benefits ran out, I fended for myself by stealing tins of spaghetti and ravioli from a local shop.

I broke the news of my pregnancy to Andy, as he and a friend made a brief visit to my flat. My announcement was clumsy. They both sneered about how I was trying to manipulate him. That was how they saw it, or at least pretended to. I was seen as the feeble girlfriend trying to rob her man of his worldly freedom, and apparently I had deliberately become pregnant to achieve this.

However, it was business as usual for Andy – while I was the one who felt trapped. Any social excitement I had gained by joining Andy's gang was about to be erased. I became the one sitting at home, while everyone else lived the life of drink, drugs and excess.

Andy did apologise for the callous comments made in his friend's company. Whenever they were present he was incapable of showing that he might care about anything other than his reputation. It was part of his image and culture, the couldn't-care-less attitude, and his mates, like his mum, were firmly placed on a pedestal. I had desperately wanted to be a part of their camaraderie and loyalty, but in truth my presence had been tolerated like a mild headache.

It was within this social circle that I told Andy I was pregnant with his child. He then told his mum, but I had yet to break the news to mine. I had, however, committed myself to keeping the baby. It was a new situation, a new relationship and, true to form, I abandoned everything else to intensify and control the single experience.

Andy visited, but he kept a strict routine that only allowed him time for a girlfriend at night. Like clockwork, he would leave his house in the afternoon, attend to whatever business he had to sort out, and make his daily visit to his mum for food. When his day was done, he would call at my place, and we would stay up until two in the morning. He once brought me some leftover shepherd's pie from his mum's table, but beyond the occasional gesture, he didn't want to look after me. He first distanced himself verbally, speaking his doubts over any future we had together. Then he distanced himself physically by letting his routine dictate his priorities. I considered myself lucky to make an appearance in his life at all.

For a while, I worked in a bakery. It provided me with a little more money and a little more food when the opportunity arose to steal some.

One day I decided to ring Mum from the shop to tell her that her youngest daughter had fallen pregnant. I remembered what had happened when my sister Marissa had become pregnant, at the age of nineteen. Mum had said, 'Whatever you want to do, I will support you. Even if you want an abortion, I will support you.'

Then there was Bev – she'd become pregnant at seventeen. She had delivered her news, defeated and crushed, and I had been deeply upset for her. Mum had cried, but vowed to support her in any way she could. Mum had been amazing.

Now it was my turn. With the memories of how she had treated my sisters, I picked up the telephone and dialled my mother's number. Mum answered the phone.

'Mum, I've got something to tell you,' I announced.

'Oh yes?'

'I'm pregnant.'

I had expected her to say how much she would support me, but instead she just said, 'Oh, really, are you?'

My heart began to sink. She sounded so unconcerned. 'Yes,' I said.

'So, what are you going to do? Are you going to keep it?'

'Yes.' By now the conversation had become painfully awkward. We both went quiet. Then Mum spoke, abruptly.

'Look, I've got to go, Mand. I can't talk now.'

The phone went dead.

Shocked, I replaced the receiver and thought about what had just happened. Mum had not been supportive, interested, cross or upset. Even if she had aired her disappointment, telling me that I could have done better, it would have been something. Instead, she'd seemed indifferent.

I avoided telling my sisters, because I was ashamed of what I saw as failure. I had proudly believed that getting pregnant like them would never happen to me, but I had been proven wrong. Still, at least if it didn't work out with Andy then I would only have the one child to contend with; I could still lead the kind of life I enjoyed.

I didn't keep the job at the bakery, so most of my pregnancy was either spent round a friend's house or stuck in front of the television. I continued to smoke and get stoned, although I managed to give up speed and acid, aided by a lack of money. Andy may not have been around to help me, but he went mad when he found out I was still smoking. But despite his nagging, I could not give it up. I was lonely and scared; it was not a great time.

When I was eight months pregnant, I attended the christening of my sister Carol's daughter. Mum was looking healthier than usual; she had lost weight and gained a boyfriend. He was married of course, and despite everything Mum had taught us, she was now convinced that he would leave his wife for her. It was upsetting to hear her proclamations of undying love. I could not believe that she had fallen for such stupid lies. Mum claimed that she had finally found happiness, but I think she had grown lonely living by herself. The control over her daughters had once empowered her, but perhaps, in her loneliness, her proud independence seemed less attractive. But it was great to see Mum that day; we seemed to get along with a new sense of ease. I have a photograph of the two of us sitting together. I am heavily pregnant, and Mum has her obligatory cigarette in hand.

In the last few weeks of my pregnancy, I tried to persuade Andy to accompany me when the time came to give birth. Instead of agreeing, he continued to remind me of our uncertain future.

One morning, I awoke around six with some peculiar pains in my tummy. I panicked and told Andy that I was going to have the baby. He got up and left the house. I had no idea where he had gone, and so I sat for another couple of hours until he returned with his parents. They were welcome strangers on that crucial morning.

'What do you want to do?' his mother asked me.

'What do you mean, what do I want to do?' I replied. 'How am I supposed to know?'

'Well, we'll stay with you, if you like – and we'll see how it goes.'

So I spent the day with Andy's parents, fantasising that I had found a new, 'proper' family to be part of. By doing the right thing for them, perhaps they would accept me. Maybe Andy would stay with me, and I would find the family that I had been searching for.

At four in the afternoon my contractions were about five minutes apart. The midwife was called. We were told to wait until they were one minute apart, and then to make our way to the hospital. I didn't understand any of this; I had received no education or advice on pregnancy, and had not attended antenatal classes. Andy's father suddenly declared that he was ready to go to the hospital now. When I protested that the pain was not that bad, I was bundled into the back of his new car and driven to the hospital. Suddenly my waters broke, but I still didn't know what was happening beyond the fact that I was making a mess of the back seat, so I kept quiet.

We arrived at the hospital around five o'clock, and I was in the most horrendous pain. I was in agony, but the nurse asked me whether I wanted a bath. This sounded like a ridiculous question because I thought I was dying, but I managed to bathe, despite vomiting. The ordeal lasted for hours, the pain almost beyond what I thought I could endure. Then, at two minutes to twelve, at last I gave birth to a baby girl.

My instinct was to look after my baby and I held her briefly, then I quickly gave her to Andy's mum. At the time I simply wanted to please; I desperately wanted to be part of a family. My baby daughter was taken away and I was woken later to feed her for the first time. We bonded throughout the night.

People I didn't know were exclaiming how well I had done. This was a strange compliment, because there had been no choice in the matter; no escape from the blood, vomit and agonising pain. The senior midwife remarked that I was coping amazingly well with motherhood, too, but due to my experience with my sisters' babies and my work as a nanny, changing and feeding a newborn had become second nature to me.

The following day I spoke to Andy's mum over the phone. She wanted to know what I was going to call the new arrival. I immediately asked her what she thought, and she confessed to liking the name Danielle; that was good enough for me.

Andy had excused himself from the birth. I had been too confused to ask for my own mum, and I didn't know the woman who had accompanied me very well, but wanted desperately to please her. The pregnancy mirrored my journey of never knowing who would be there for me, and so I reached blindly for the nearest friendly face. However, amid all the disorder and chaos, I had stumbled upon a rare achievement. I may have been robbed of the encouragement and love of my mum, but Danielle, meaning 'God is judge', was my daughter.

6

Revolving Doors

Having to expose Danielle to a world in which I struggled to survive, filled me with dread. So showing off my new baby was a nice distraction from those dark fears.

My first visitors to the maternity ward were Mum, Carol and Lynn. I was overjoyed to see them, and keen to show them their newborn grandchild and niece. Mum saw little resemblance between Danielle and I, but said that she was tiny and beautiful.

I remember looking in Mum's eyes and noticing that they were yellow. She explained that she had actually come from the hospital herself because she had been undergoing tests. The doctors thought she had yellow jaundice, but she said not to worry. Before leaving, Mum asked why I had not called her earlier. I felt ashamed, but I couldn't explain my reasons or behaviour.

Amazingly, Andy visited, arriving with the two girls I had shared a house with. He sat on the bed looking uneasy. But despite his fears, he offered his daughter a genuine father's touch. This made me extremely happy, and the following day my two old housemates returned to take me home.

While in the safety of the hospital, I had been confident with the initial challenges of motherhood. But now I had to face those deep concerns about bringing up Danielle in such a cold world. On the way home from hospital, my old housemates admitted to confronting Andy to persuade him to visit. I was grateful for their efforts, because Andy had allowed himself a brief respite from his selfish bravado.

About two weeks before my stay in hospital, and with no guarantee that he even wanted to be with me any more, we had moved into a one-bedroom flat together. When I returned to the flat, I was left alone with my baby. My belongings had yet to be unpacked, but I had prepared a space especially for tiny Danielle. People provided clothes for her and made sure that I had everything I needed. Back on benefits, the money had doubled and my rent was being paid as well. Andy eventually showed up at the flat and promptly told me off for smoking. He was right, and so I took my habit into the kitchen. From there I could smoke with the window open. When Andy's parents arrived, the first thing they did was offer their opinion on the matter. Having felt initially confident as a new mother, I was now surrounded by people who could only point out what I was doing wrong. They never once encouraged me in what I was actually trying to get right.

I wanted to befriend Andy's parents. Not only were they Danielle's grandparents, but also Andy was far from supportive. He showed little interest in the benefits of family, and so I visited them almost every day without him. Andy's mum doted on Danielle. She was as excited as I was about every glimmer of Danielle's innocence, and I loved this. Unfortunately her excitement was matched only by her fanatical criticism of my every breath as a young mother. Her comments left me feeling raw and angry. I was told how they were making a special allowance for my age. It was not easy being a mother at eighteen – raising and loving a child is a huge responsibility at any age – and being treated like a child only made it harder.

About a week after Danielle was born, Mum came to see me at the flat. It was around midday. We got on really well – and then she asked where Andy was. I told her that he was still in bed.

'Right,' said Mum. 'I'm going to see him.' And she marched into the bedroom as Andy pulled the covers over his head.

'Andy, this is my mum,' I said, weakly. 'Please just say hello.'

He grunted from under the blankets.

Mum never stood for rudeness. She reminded him of the correct way to greet people and left him to his hibernation.

'I hope I haven't landed you in trouble,' she told me. She'd evidently guessed that Andy was not always the gentlest of creatures.

'No,' I said. 'He's the one who's in trouble, because nobody talks to you like that and gets away with it!' I was furious with Andy; I could not believe that he could be so lazy and rude. I had developed a new bond with Mum since the christening. Andy's selfishness was not going to rob me of this overdue relationship.

The following day I received another visit, this time from my sister Carol and her husband. Having seen Mum the previous day, I already suspected what Carol had come to tell me.

'Mum's got cancer.'

Somehow, I'd been expecting that news. However, it was still devastating.

I packed a bag and left Andy a note which said that Mum had cancer and that Danielle and I were staying in

Eastbourne. Carol drove me to my eldest sister Lynn's house. I gave her Danielle, and then we made our way to the hospital to see Mum. It had only been a couple of weeks since I'd left hospital with my new baby. Now I was spun right around and thrown straight back through its revolving doors.

When we found Mum's ward, she sat up to greet us. Even in the hospital, she still had her packet of cigarettes next to her. The only words I could find to say were, 'I love you, Mum,' and I repeated them over and over. We had been told that she had around three months to live. I talked about her getting better, so that we could all go on holiday together. But as I voiced all my plans for Mum's recuperation, Mum turned to my sister and said, 'You did tell her, didn't you, Carol?'

'Yes, she did,' I said. 'I know, Mum, I know you're ill, but you might get better long enough for us to do these things.'

It was a difficult and desperate conversation with a dying woman.

The day after our first visit, we had an appointment with the consultant. All five sisters sat uncomfortably in a small room, waiting for some glimmer of light and hope. Mum was due to have an operation that after-noon, which could prolong her life, but there were no certainties – in fact there was only a fifty-fifty chance of survival. We were advised to go home and wait by the phone. They would contact us regarding any further developments.

I wish I had remained by Mum's side. But it was all so surreal that I could only drift along, carried and tossed by a helpless urgency. Between us we made a decision that we could not all say our goodbyes at once. Marissa and I saw Mum together, and once again I had nothing to say apart from how much I loved her. Having said goodbye, we returned home and waited for the hospital to ring. When we were still waiting long into the evening, we decided to ring them. We were told that the doctors had changed their minds; the operation had not taken place. In hindsight, I suspect this to have been Mum's decision. I knew that she would have been worried about us; she often said she never wanted to be a burden to anyone. Mum had extensive experience in mental hospitals and nursing homes, cleaning and spoon-feeding the incontinent and those unable to help themselves. Mum did not want to be in that position. She used to tell us that she would rather die at the age of sixty than risk getting any older. I believe that when the doctors had explained that there was a possibility of prolonging her life, Mum declined the opportunity. To Mum, life had been nothing but hardship and pain. I don't think she had the desire to fight on any longer.

After the emotional drama of the hospital failing to ring us, Lynn decided that if Mum was going to die, then it would happen at home surrounded by her daughters. The Bryan Adams song 'Everything I Do, I Do it for You' was number one in the UK music charts. Lynn took a copy of the song and a Walkman into hospital for Mum. On our following visit, Mum said that she had tried to listen to it, but had started to cry, and people had been watching. Even though she had given up the fight to live, she was still determined to appear strong and resilient.

Mum was taken to Lynn's place. It was a massive, three-storey townhouse, where the smell of percolated coffee and roast dinners would often greet your arrival. Everything was just right in her home. And Lynn had turned one of her nice reception rooms into a bedroom for Mum.

I returned to Worthing to collect baby necessities for Danielle. There was not much I could do for Mum, except occasionally wash her hair. Mum spent her time composing individual photo albums for us all.

Having already asked my sisters, Mum asked me whether there was anything I wanted to know before she died. I believe wholeheartedly that had I asked, Mum would have told me all about the father I never had. But at the time, I could not focus beyond the mother I was about to lose, and so I said 'No.'

I wanted to reassure Mum that we all loved her, even though some of us could only express this through absence. I could empathise with their decision; watching Mum waste away to a skeleton was distressing for the entire family.

At this time, Nan came to stay. She and Mum slept in the same room, and Mum received her first proper night's sleep for months. Over the years, their own relationship had also been strained and damaged. Was this because Nan was a churchgoer, and didn't approve of her daughter's lifestyle? I don't know. But right then, Nan's company and compassion had miraculously brought a healing between them, and I believe it allowed Mum a glimpse of peace.

The days rolled into one at Lynn's home. I would lay Danielle on the bed next to Mum while she slept. They both appeared as frail as each other. But as Danielle's life was beautifully soft and full of hope, Mum's was brittle and rapidly fading away.

One day, most of the family had gathered at the house. Despite falling in and out of sleep, Mum was in good spirits. She spoke to us through her heavy, rattling breath.

'I'm so pleased you are all here,' she said.

'How are you, Pam?' my sister's husband asked her.

'I'm fine, actually,' she smiled. 'I was going to ask you for a dance!' They both laughed. But I knew Mum was just trying to make him feel more comfortable.

Then, as I was bathing Danielle, I heard frantic voices shouting to phone a doctor. Mum had stopped breathing and the house was filled with pandemonium. I ran to join my sisters, and Nan took Danielle from me in case I dropped her in the commotion. When I saw Mum lying motionless, I started screaming. Carol told me to stop being hysterical, and so Marissa and I ran upstairs.

'Why Mum?' I kept saying. As an older sister, Marissa felt she should comfort me – even in her own pain. We hugged and cried together, until the doctor arrived to confirm that Mum had died.

During the night, I had to find a baby bottle for Danielle. I ventured down into the kitchen where Mum's body had been placed. It was strange knowing and feeling so much love for Mum, only to be frightened and repelled by her dead body. The following morning she was taken away, and Pam Curtis physically left our world forever.

Her dance with life had ended.

7

Strangely Numb

I watched the curtains close over her coffin. It was a sombre and heavy occasion, steeped in tradition and ceremony. Around thirty people were present as Mum was cremated. How sad it was to witness all that her life had amounted to. She had attracted so little love. I reflected on her life and the fact that she had never known her father; how had that really affected her, I wondered . . . The Bryan Adams song was played. It had remained in the charts for the entire duration of Mum's hospital stay, and left the charts on the week of the funeral.

After I had left home, as the last of her dependants, Mum had moved to a smaller rented flat. On the news of her death, the owners demanded that we cleared out her belongings to make room for their new tenants. I became angry at what appeared to be the callousness of people. I wanted to explain to strangers what had happened, to shout about my loss to people in the street. I became very aware of other people and how they too could be handling and hiding fragile hearts.

My old school friend, Lisa, attended the funeral. Seeing her again was a delight, which alleviated some of the tension of the day. The wake was held at Lynn's house, and I remember seeing the familiar faces of Lisa's mother and Mum's old neighbour from the green. Lisa invited me back to her house for the night and I accepted. Her mum looked after our baby daughters and we were temporarily released from our responsibilities as young mothers.

Our first port of call was the local drug dealer, where we bought some LSD. We had no idea where we wanted to go – I just wanted an effective escape from the way I was feeling. We ventured out to revisit what felt like better times, and called at an old friend's house where I was surprised to see another childhood friend, my neighbour, Alan.

'It's really good to see you, Mandy,' he said. 'I'm really sorry to hear about your mum. I would've liked to have come to the funeral.' It came flooding back – how much he and his brother had meant to me.

'It's lovely to be with you, too. It's wonderful to be back,' I replied. I gave him a big hug. We looked at the surroundings and remembered how as kids we all used to play there together. There were so many memories.

Seeing Alan, Lisa and old faces from the small town near Eastbourne where I'd grown up reminded me of the days on the green. For a brief moment I felt comforted – it was like receiving a postcard from somewhere far away but ever familiar.

The next day, Carol drove me back to Worthing. I sat in the car and watched the world go by. It dawned on me that I would never make another journey to see Mum. Even attending her funeral had been an act of wanting to do something to please her. The whirlwind of the hospital, Mum, and the funeral came to a halt, leaving me shattered, totally devoid of feeling.

Back in Worthing, Andy was initially supportive – he even put his arms around me. But as we lay in bed that

night, he announced that there was something important he had to tell me. In my absence, he had been paying another girl some attention. It was not as though he
had even felt bad about it – he had simply missed being
the emotional focus of my life. I didn't feel anything, and
I knew that it was only a matter of time before I left him.

For a while, I suffered from nightmares. Expecting a
visit from a little girl, I would hear a knock at the door.
When I answered it, all I saw was Mum's dead face.
Witnessing death had frightened me. The contrast of
Danielle's birth followed by Mum's death became emotionally overwhelming. I became dependent on dope
again; anything to shield the mess and ease the cutting
edge of reality.

Andy only smoked when he drank. When he drank,
he binged, and when he binged he sometimes took pills
as well. He never smoked in the flat, and he hated the
fact that I did. I didn't smoke much during the day, but
as soon as Danielle was safe in bed, my aim was to get
as stoned as possible. It became an increasingly lonely
practise. The flat began to resemble a prison in which I,
a young single mum, had become the sole inmate.
Sitting by the window became my silent plea for somebody to save me from this world. I had once dreamt that
when the pregnancy was over I would regain my life,
and Andy's parents would take an active role in helping.
But when they did take an interest, I felt it was completely over the top. I also felt that they thought I should
be eternally grateful for any effort they made as doting
grandparents.

Andy and I lived together, but we had different lives.
I went to bed early because Danielle woke up early.
Meanwhile, Andy stuck to his routine of surfacing from
bed at around two in the afternoon. Then he went to the
pub and I knew I wouldn't see him again until late. We

rarely communicated; our already poor relationship was fast deteriorating.

I remember not quite cooking some pork chops to his liking. He threw his plate at the wall, plunging into absolute rage.

'These chops are raw!' he bellowed, filling the air with filthy language. 'I just want to kill you, you useless . . .'

It was as though a switch had been flicked inside his head, turning him from a man into an animal. I was frozen with fear, not wanting to move or say a word. But in my mind I was crying out for my mum. I wanted her more than ever.

Andy gained great satisfaction from playing mind games. People had warned me about him in the pub, saying that he would push me to the limit until I could not take any more. This was Andy's way of controlling people – through fear. He told me that the only way he had coped in prison was to pretend that he was a mad-man, which protected him from the real madmen. I don't know to what extent Andy was in control when he lost his temper, but something in his eyes hinted that it wasn't just a game.

We moved again, this time to a larger two-bedroom flat. There was no garden, and the way through the maisonette was up a narrow flight of stairs. The grey rooms with black coving and shabby brown carpet did not make it feel inviting – neither did the *Hell Raiser* movie poster on the wall. But at least there was the potential of a fresh start.

One of Andy's friends lived downstairs, so the building was full of activity, with people coming and going. I was excited at the prospect of meeting new people and regaining a social life. But I soon felt the lonely sting of what became my new prison. All I had achieved was a change of cells – the walls and the bars remained the same. My survival tactics were to get as stoned as possible every night, smoking one joint after another. By half past nine I was capable of nothing but drug-induced sleep. Watching endless television became my only real pleasure, because the drugs had become a necessity rather than an enjoyable social pursuit.

If I knew Andy was going out, I occasionally chose a video from the rental shop down the road. It wasn't long before I stopped. The man who worked there told me how Andy had paid him a paranoid visit, warning him not to talk to me. This was typical of Andy. When we first met, if I ever spoke to any of his friends in the pub, he would sneer that I fancied them. It acted as a sly verbal warning to both parties – and he wasn't averse to threatening his friends in the pub toilets, either. I had once enjoyed the company of his friends, but they'd soon learned to avoid me.

I began to attend a Mums and Toddlers group. They met in the community hall across the road and called themselves 'Crafty Mums'. The idea was to bring along a leisure activity, while the volunteers attended to the kids in the crèche. These moments of social contact became heaven for me. I found company among the other mothers, as well as receiving a break from Danielle. The Crafty Mums were a warm and welcoming group of women. Most of them were Christians who attended the local Elim church, but I didn't feel threatened by this. In fact, as I listened to them, it soon struck me that they were far from perfect, and I liked that.

My only experience of church had been during Mum's brief involvement with the Mormons. I had accompanied Mum while she attended their services for a while. Whenever they sent their people to visit the house, Mum would panic, stop swearing, hide the cigarettes under the sofa, and spray her house and children with air freshener. She would snatch our cigarettes away, and even go as far as throwing her tea down the drain, which I found hilarious. It was as though the religious police had arrived at our door. Mum's sudden façade of decaffeinated living was for their benefit alone. They promoted their beliefs to Mum, and Mum performed her act for them; neither party was any the wiser.

Bev and I found their visits exciting because they were American, and it was fun listening to their accents. They gave us a bit of attention, which we were forever craving. They were too perfect though, too 'by the book', appearing trapped by rigorous standards of procedure. I could not imagine for one second that God, if he was real, judged us on our caffeine intake, or on how many rules were enforced to disinfect our lives.

By contrast, the Crafty Mums group were far more approachable. They didn't elevate themselves as being too spiritual for the world. I met a lady there called Jenny Quaif who was looking for a childminder. I had already fallen in love with her beautiful baby daughter, and because I wanted Danielle to be around other children, I offered my services based on my experience as a nanny. I spent three days a week childminding for Jenny, and it provided me with some extra cash, most of which was spent on dope.

The situation at home worsened. One night, when Danielle and I were trying sleep, Andy invited his friends home. Throughout the early hours of the morning, the walls shook with the repetitive thud of his mindless rave music. Pleading with him to turn it down for Danielle's sake, I received a volley of threats and obscenities. When his drunken friends finally left, Andy exploded with rage. He became primeval due to whisky and drugs. Andy had never hit me, but he would run at me and press his fist into my face. It was terrifying because I feared the fist becoming a punch, and thought that if it ever did, then the punches might never stop.

The threats became so severe that I would run from the house to find somewhere else to stay, sometimes even leaving Danielle behind to save myself. Deep down, something told me that, despite all his threats, Andy would never actually hurt Danielle. Despite my desire to pack my bags for Eastbourne, I could not sever Danielle's chance at a relationship with her father. Andy exploited this as my weakness. He threatened to leave and never see Danielle again, but this was his most empty of threats, because he loved his daughter too much.

I began to feel suffocated every time Andy came near me, and I would do anything to avoid sleeping with him. Whereas previously in life I had worn the appropriate mask to endure sex, now the mask had slipped and I could no longer hide my disgust. I was nineteen, with a baby daughter, trapped in a loveless relationship and I wanted to die. One day, I forgot to take my contraceptive pill, and to my horror I discovered that I was pregnant again.

I had carried a secret hope born from romantic movies that I would meet my dream guy and live happily ever after. The thought of having two children with Andy diminished this hope. I had a grim picture of never leaving him, for the children's sake. I visited the doctor. This time there was no wrestling with the decision. Not under any circumstances would I keep the baby. The doctor wanted to make sure that I was clear-minded, and I gave him an entire list of reasons to satisfy him. Andy treated me badly. I didn't want to be in the relationship, and I was leaving at the first opportunity. In the light of these revelations, I was told that I was wise.

But if I had been so wise, the situation would never have existed in the first place.

On the morning of the abortion I told Andy where I was going.

'I don't think I can keep this baby,' I told him. 'I want to have an abortion.'

'It's your decision,' said Andy, 'you're the one who has to look after it.'

So that was it. That was the sum total of our conversation. It was the start of a long, lonely journey to the hospital.

I arrived at the same place where I had given birth to my daughter. But this time it looked different. I gave my name to the receptionist and was escorted to an isolated room, where I was left on my own. But the only thing I could think of was that I hadn't brought a spare pair of knickers with me. When a nurse came, I attempted a conversation. I was really after some guidance.

'What do you think about what I am doing?' I asked.

'We are not meant to give our opinion,' she responded. But it was obvious from her look that she did not approve of my actions.

I was wheeled down to an operating theatre in a solemn, silent procession. I had a mask put over me, and was told to count to ten. The next thing I remember was waking up among a row of other patients. I had told myself that I wasn't losing a baby, but fixing a problem. However, now my body, heart and soul were strangely numb, and I felt more depressed than ever.

8

Death Sentence

I don't know where I found the strength. I rang Andy and gave him an ultimatum. Either he left the flat allowing me to return – after which he could see Danielle at weekends – or I would stay in Eastbourne, and he would never see the two of us again.

He laughed, but agreed to leave so that I could come back to Worthing. I returned to the flat as Andy was clearing out his belongings. Again he laughed, asking me why I was behaving so melodramatically. He failed to understand. He had drummed into me so often that I would never cope without him, because I was nothing but a useless piece of rubbish. It was Andy who ended up believing it. He left, the flat was mine, and I had finally found my freedom.

For the last year of our relationship, I had mentally prepared myself for this separation. When my life began again, I was neither upset nor missing Andy. I felt fantastic, free from fear and persecution. However, being single left a void. And into that void I poured my desperation to fulfil my romantic fantasy.

It was not long before I met somebody else, and this time my affections were reciprocated. But Andy was far from being a mere ghost of a memory. In my foolishness, I casually mentioned my new boyfriend within earshot of one of Andy's mates. My new man was issued with a warning by Andy's friends, along with a curt reminder of how their leader dealt with such problems. Our relationship ended as quickly as it had begun, and so too did my dream of freedom. I realised that in Andy's eyes I was still his property. I was branded by the mark of his name and ruined by the stigma of his reputation.

Andy's presence was far more than a dark cloud over my life. He regularly banged on the doors and windows trying to enter my flat. I relocated again, this time to a two-bedroom house with a back garden, which was perfect for Danielle. The house would only be mine on payment of a £400 deposit. My friendship with Jenny Quaif from the Mums' group became a blessing. I could comfortably ask for financial help without her feeling obliged or offended. We reached an agreement where she would pay my deposit, and I would work for her for two months with no wages. She became my guarantor, agreeing to cover my rent if ever the day came when I could not afford to pay it myself. When I moved in, I told Jenny what a godsend she had been. Although it was a figure of speech, part of me wanted it to be literal. Jenny simply smiled.

One night I was out on the town in Worthing with Jenny's older daughter. We bumped into Andy in one of the town pubs. He interrogated me, trying to steal the evening. The questions spilled out from his suspicious mind until Jenny's daughter told him to leave us alone. She knew of Andy, but had no idea what he was really like beyond his shadowy reputation. Her rebuke was well-intentioned but misinformed. Instead of it being a refreshing denouncement of my past, it only served to remind me of how close and dangerous Andy still was. I had not broken free from his chains yet.

Jenny's daughter stayed the night, and because we were friends there was no problem with her sleeping in the same bed. In the middle of the night Andy burst into the room like the Special Forces.

'I've caught you, you slag!'

When both our heads shot up from the covers he became very apologetic. He may have been suspicious and controlling, calling me everything from stupid to ugly, but in his absence, I was not about to become a lesbian. He thought he had caught me with a man, but as soon as he saw Jenny's daughter, he disappeared like a snake back into the darkness. I shuddered to think what might have happened if I had been with a boyfriend. I was relieved more than worried, but Jenny's daughter had feared the worst. Her terrified reaction illustrated how conditioned I had become to accepting this kind of behaviour as normal.

I had genuinely believed that leaving Andy would give me a new lightness of spirit. Unfortunately, he still treated me as he pleased, with no respect for my feelings and no recognition of my independence from him. I had no hope of meeting anybody else. Whenever I did, they were quickly warned away by Andy's spies. But I couldn't move away; the thing that kept me in Worthing was my stubborn determination not to take Danielle away from her father. I could not do it. I had never known my father, and thought I never would, but Danielle would know hers, no matter what.

Andy and Danielle saw each other every other weekend, and I was grateful for this. It helped to give me a break from single parenthood, although without Danielle the loneliness only grew stronger. To get through this, I smoked ever-increasing amounts of dope, funded by my childminding duties plus my child benefit. I took speed as well, which helped me to cope with the housework.

I wasn't any happier for leaving Andy, but I knew it would be the wrong move to accept him back. In drunken outbursts, he began hammering on the front door, trying to break in again. But on other occasions, he was relaxed and friendly. I never knew which side of him I was going to witness. He could be caring, only to suddenly fly into fits of abuse. We were so incompatible that we drove each other mad, but I felt a deep and terrible guilt for leaving him. I wanted nothing more than for him to meet somebody else. Maybe then I could allow myself to be truly free.

An old friend and neighbour asked me if I could look after her little girl. I was already looking after Danielle and two of Jenny's children and so I said 'Yes'. It was the social link that I needed, because all Andy's friends had deserted me to follow their captain. This woman introduced me to a man named Darren. We had met once before when he had enjoyed flirting with me in front of Andy, which had made my ex seethe with fury. Darren was the only person I knew who could get away with this, because his reputation was more psychopathic than Andy's. While Andy was lazy and apathetic, Darren was emotional and passionate. He had a penchant for really skinny women, and I only weighed seven stone. I preferred smoking to eating. The only time I ever felt hungry was when my mind was blurred and bruised by dope.

I went out with Darren and we stayed up all night talking and laughing. He respected Andy as a fellow hard man, and by their 'code of honour' he should not have been dating a mate's ex-girlfriend. However, these rules appeared to be honoured at the individual's discretion. He neither feared Andy, nor worried about any reprisals over his skinny new girlfriend. While he thought that he was madly in love with me, I was buzzing about my new man, believing that I had found true happiness.

Despite Andy's objections and disgust at Darren's disloyalty, Darren stayed, and life was enjoyable for a couple of months. But like all my relationships, the honeymoon period faded, and our joint insecurities left two sets of heavy luggage at our door. Darren's routine was disturbingly similar to Andy's. He disappeared every night and then climbed in through the window at two in the morning. There were rumours of him with other girls, perhaps climbing in and out of other windows. Unsurprisingly, I found it hard to sustain any physical affection for him. And in the midst of yet another failing relationship, disaster struck again: I became pregnant.

The horror of ending up like Mum hit me hard. I could not live my life, single to the last, with a family of children all by different fathers. But I was 'lucky' because society granted me the right to abort any unwanted baby, and so I paid another visit to the same doctor as before. This time the advice he gave me was different.

'Start saying "No"!'

This simple little word had remained firmly outside my strength and experience. After all, weren't women, like men, supposed to be used for sex? If so, then why should I think of myself as being any different to Mum?

The second abortion was handled at a private clinic, and Darren paid the fee. I knew that our relationship would end as a result of this. Darren wanted to travel; he often told me that he had a great plan and to watch how his dreams would come true. In truth, he drove a van for a couple of thieves while they stole from the elderly with their scams and con tricks. One day I received a visit from the local heavy mob. They voiced their 'concern' over Darren's whereabouts and I was told that he had left the country with some of their money. That had been his great plan. He may not have said goodbye, but at least there was absolutely no hope of him ever returning. That particular fantasy ended there.

All these relationships felt like a brief taste, sweet but then bitter, of a dream I could never live. One dream crashed and another arrived to take its place. I believed that each new encounter would ease the pain of the previous disaster. But it ultimately rubbed salt into the same open wound.

I was a lonely girl, clinging to other people for security. Some fill their own voids with careers and family; others with reputations, violence, sex, and drugs. I merely wanted to be loved and valued. It was what I had always wanted, right from the time I was a little girl on the green. I needed love, but I didn't know what it was. Was it love which desired me one minute, only to chase me down the street wanting to smash my face in the next? Was it love which promised intimacy, but thirsted for sex? The pain and loneliness became unbearable. Once again I sat by the window watching the world pass me by, longing for someone to knock on my door and extend a saving hand. I hated myself and wanted to be any one of the passing strangers beyond the windowpane. I felt my life should have been like gold, but everything I touched turned to rubbish. I even cried to Andy, asking why these things kept happening to me.

Andy was still a part of my life, and his relationship with Danielle was good. I remained determined that she would not be brought up seeing her parents screaming at each other. But there was a terrible clash of worlds between us; Andy had been taught to treat women like trash, to 'treat them mean and keep them keen'. He was taught to break a woman into submission, and I had once been close to fitting that mould. On the other hand, I had grown up listening to Mum's equally distorted view, which was never to let a man lead you, even on small issues. Both perspectives were wrong. One was a blatant disrespect for women and the other, a cold and hard suspicion of men. They were two extremes with no understanding of how to meet in the middle; any attempts would result in disaster.

My will to continue to fight began to wither, and I became a pale shadow of the woman I longed to be. I saw my old housemates, the two girls who had once driven me home from hospital with my newborn Danielle. They asked me whether I would attend a keep fit class with them. I missed dancing, and longed for the freedom where I had once flourished. It was so exciting to be going out with people, and they agreed to pick me up. It was a few days before my twenty-first birthday. Andy said he would look after Danielle while I went out, but he failed to turn up and so I couldn't go. The walls closed in around me. When the girls arrived, I opened the door and collapsed on my knees in front of them, sobbing like a child. I pleaded for their help because I felt like I was losing my mind. I didn't know what to do any more and I wanted to die. As I cried on my knees in a shameless display of despair, they said they would return to see how I was after their class had finished. The hours dragged on and the doorbell remained deafeningly silent. When they failed to return, the rejection tipped the scales.

The day before my birthday I gave Andy some money to buy my dope. I was now completely dependent on it to sleep, having become paranoid and jumpy from spending too much time alone. The house was a dark cage in which I listened for noises and feared what might be staring back at me through the bars. There were times when I thought I saw demons at the door, and maybe I did. Drugs had become malignant, feeding my sickness. I was isolated and afraid, held captive by my own fear.

My emotions were raw. Another birthday was about to mark yet another useless anniversary of my life. I distrusted people and I was disgusted with humanity and my place in it. There was a hole in my heart, once occupied by Mum, but the hole had become bigger than the shape she had left. It was a gaping chasm from which voices insulted and laughed at me. As I waited for my drugs, Andy failed to show up for the second time that week. I finally resigned myself to bed, knowing that there was no fix to help me sleep.

That night, it felt like my heart had been gashed and broken. There was nothing I could do to stop the bleeding. The pain and rejection were too much to bear and I cried again, pounding my fists on the bed. I should have been learning all the joys of life, but instead every negative word that had been spoken about me – useless, stupid, thick, ugly, pathetic, worthless – bore down on me with a ruthless ferocity. I had been the girl who'd wanted to make something of herself. I'd listened instead to the criticism of the world, and accepted its appalling judgement. I was nothing, and I was ready to die.

Plans of suicide buzzed around my aching head, and I sifted through them. I worked out that by ringing a particular phone number by a particular time, perhaps somebody would respond. This was for Danielle's sake. By that time, my own pain would be over. My daughter would be safe and I would be dead. Again the pain welled up, but this time I didn't cry to myself, I couldn't, there was nothing left of me. And so I cried out to God. Through utter fear, desperation, and contempt for the world I cried, 'If there is a God, then you have to help me, because I can't cope any longer. I can't do it. If this is all there is, then I don't want it any more!'

And then, at the most catastrophic and suicidal point of my life, at my weakest and most vulnerable, forming my plans of suicide, I felt a tremendous peace sweep over me. It invaded my life, saturating my heart and mind. It took away every painful insult and incision. In fact, it was more than peace. It was a profound joy that I had not felt before: the pure but alien joy of simply being alive. I was completely overwhelmed and so I asked, sheepishly, 'Is this God?' And as I did, I was answered by the sound of the letterbox. I jumped out of bed, and from the window I saw a lady from the Mums' group leaving in her car. Downstairs, lying by the door was a birthday card from her family. Written at the bottom was an invitation to come to church the following morning.

I could not believe it, and I laughed with excitement, because only minutes before I had been on the brink of suicide. I lay my head on the pillow and thought, *OK, it looks like I'm going to church tomorrow*, and as soon as I made that decision, another river of peace flowed through me. With no dope to smoke and no tears to cry, I fell asleep without another thought of the terror I had experienced. For once it was peace that allowed me to sleep, rather than pain which had sentenced me to death. But was this peace from God?

I was about to find out.

Part II

A New Path

9

New Day

All I could do was laugh. For instead of the heaviness and despair of having to face my daily routine, I felt the joy of living. It was my twenty-first birthday, and I had woken up to the sound of the birds singing outside. But now I actually stopped to listen. It was a new day unlike any other.

Remembering the events of the night before, I prepared myself for church and dressed Danielle. The happiness of the occasion washed through me. I had something to do and somewhere to go. Amazingly, the peace from the preceding night had not left me; it was sustaining me and urging me forwards. There was actually life outside of my emotional coma.

The church was called Elim, a strange name for a church. The congregation met in a hall hired from the local Catholic girls' school, but I was to find that Elim was not a place of high religion. It was an evangelical church, very free in character. In my mind I ran through all the people I knew, wondering what on earth they would say if they could see what I was doing. What would Andy and his friends think, seeing me walk into this old school hall where people met to worship God?

For most of my life, Sunday morning had indeed been sacred – it was reserved for sleeping off hangovers from the night before.

As I entered the building, I noticed that there were no pews; neither was there any grand architecture. This was not what I was expecting. I found a chair facing the stage and as the proceedings began, I sang along with the congregation. Danielle was frightened by the noise and started to cry. But a lady called Callie – the woman who had posted my birthday card – picked her up and kept Danielle distracted for my sake. I sang along with the others and tears fell down my face.

I listened to a lady speak about not using God's name in vain, and I was very puzzled by this. In my world I used the words 'God' and 'Jesus', so that I could swear in front of Danielle without being obscene. It was an acceptable habit to use the name of Jesus Christ as an expletive, and it wasn't something that I had ever questioned. However, there had been times when my own name had meant little more than dirt to people. Maybe cursing God's name was just as offensive or even upsetting to him.

On that Sunday morning in the school hall, God's name was lifted up far beyond any ignorant obscenity. People raised their hands and voices and brought their lives before him. For my part, I sang and cried, listened and reflected. I didn't know what to expect and I understood little of what was being said, but the same peace from the previous night was present in that building. I cried new tears, reacting to the peace rather than the pain.

As the people worshipped, I felt no embarrassment standing among the crowd. Rather than singing morose songs about God, these people sang intimate songs to him. There was an air of celebration as they sang with energy and excitement. I soaked up the atmosphere. I could have held on to my fears and doubts, folding my arms and condemning it all as nonsense, but I found myself singing. As I did, I felt something being released inside me, something deeper than I understood. I didn't know God; I didn't know Jesus. I knew he had been born in a manger and some wise men brought him some gifts, but beyond the story of the Nativity, Jesus had never mattered to me. However, these people clearly knew something that I didn't. Feeling this great sense of peace, beyond daydream and dope, I wanted more of whatever had found me in my grief; more of whatever had brought me to this meeting, however strange and unfamiliar it seemed.

I had been surprised by church, especially by seeing people my own age. The ladies from the Mums' group were all middle-aged and middle-class. I was curious to know what brought this younger and less refined crowd to church. They looked cool enough, but there was nothing fashionable about what they were doing. It was hard to comprehend that there were people my own age who were doing this, but I thought maybe some of them had stories similar to mine. I wanted to find out and so their presence became an added attraction. I decided to return to church to see what it could offer me.

My world began to change from the one I had always known. When I was at church I cried, but it wasn't the harrowing cry from my childhood. I had grown up to accept the physical pain of crying, but this was different. The process was described by the pastor of the church as being like a washing machine full of dirty laundry. What has endlessly been churned and tossed around in dirty water was now being removed one piece at a time. Every Sunday morning I began to feel this happen. A little bit more of that stained and filthy laundry was removed, and another piece of my life was set free. The long process of releasing these tattered fragments had begun.

The immediate effects of this became evident in my relationship with Danielle. During pregnancy, I had clung to the hope that Danielle alone would bring me happiness and fulfilment. She did bring me joy, but in my wounded, self-absorbed world, I could not reciprocate it. When I tried to give something back, all that spilled out was the dirt chugging around inside of me. I had applied my trophy cabinet of insecurities to Danielle's life, just as Mum had once applied hers to mine. My fear, depression and constant loneliness had so far dictated my role as a mother. This process of slowly restoring my sense of value allowed me to give some of my love back to Danielle. I felt a new freedom to be the mother that I had always wanted to be: patient, kind and loving.

On one occasion when I got a lift home in Jenny's car, she started telling me about a teaching programme run by the church.

'Would you like to meet up with me,' she asked, 'and I could take you through the basics of Christianity?'

'Yeah, that would be great,' I said. I always felt privileged that people would want to spend time with me in this way.

'I've bought a Bible for you, too,' Jenny added. 'I suggest that you read the New Testament first.'

I knew nothing of the Bible. But as I began to read it, I reflected on the change in my life. I had received an enveloping peace when I felt my life was all but over. The same night, I also received an invitation to church. I had cried in church and felt a release from my choking pain. Now my relationship with my two-year-old daughter had taken on a refreshing new lease of life.

These were facts, and so I looked at this book with eyes hungry for something more than fiction.

I found out that Christians claim that the Bible is the inspired Word of God, and that they believe it is God's account of his relationship and history with the human race he created. I flicked through its pages, and began to read the Gospel of Matthew in the New Testament. I wasn't a reader at all – I liked watching Hollywood romances – but it soon struck me that I was reading far more than a collection of obscure and wholesome teachings. I read about how Jesus intervened on behalf of a woman who'd been caught sleeping with someone who wasn't her husband. She was about to be stoned to death, but Jesus challenged the crowd to only throw the first stone if they could find no fault in themselves. They dropped the stones, and Jesus forgave the woman. To me, reading the Bible was like watching a movie – I never realised that such an old book could be such a good read. I thought *Go for it!* He was wonderful, and I loved how he responded to what moved him. It was obvious that he loved friends and enemies alike. But was far from the wishy-washy and selfish statements of love that people I knew lived by. I noticed that Jesus was also grieved and angered by the world he lived in. He loved everybody, but it appeared that society's outcasts and underdogs had a special place in his heart.

I had not decided to follow Jesus for the rest of my life, and I didn't understand anything about the cross and Jesus' death. It just seemed to me that Jesus loved the world despite all its violence, sickness and pain, and I recognised myself as being part of that pain. Therefore, he must love me too. When I went to church, his peace was there for me. However, there were nagging doubts and warnings playing on in the back of my mind.

I thought about times when I had gone with Mum to the Mormon Church. They claimed to be the true church in the name and authority of Jesus Christ, but I had found their proceedings heavy. There was no release, only shame. I remembered the conditions they had tried to impose on Mum, but saw that Jesus didn't teach this. He did not give people checklists of things to correct that made their lives more palatable. He asked people to come to him, and let him be their strength.

Another barrier to be broken was the influence of Mum's teachings. She had held onto a flimsily applied belief, adopted from watching television illusionists, that the power of the mind alone could overcome anything. Mum's influence, like the Mormon Church, tainted my first steps with God. I began to worry. Maybe people projecting the same thoughts could create the vibe and energy that I felt at church – even the presence of that wonderful peace. It sounded like a cheap answer though. No matter how much the power of the mind had been applied, there were segments of my life that simply refused to change. So despite these early worries, the real test for me was not about which church was valid, or whether the peace was from God. It was whether God really was powerful enough to change my life. Could he undo the damage I had inflicted upon myself?

Even while reading the Bible and learning how to pray, I was still addicted to smoking dope. Drugs and relationships had been the fixed pattern of my life so far.

I started going out with one of the boys from church, thinking that it would be safe because Christians are encouraged not to have sex before marriage. I had gone from one extreme to the other. For here was a young man who wouldn't hold hands in church – because his arms were raised in the air! He even blocked my attempts to kiss him after the service.

My new friend invited me to a Christian meeting. It sounded like a good idea, and so, with a car full of young enthusiasts, we set off along the south coast to an Elim Church conference.

Church had not yet become a totally joyful occasion for me. Every Sunday I was up at the front seeking prayer because I only ever saw my ugly side. I didn't feel worthy enough to be there and I cried every time I felt God's peace. Each week I would look at the pastor or any other man standing at the front, and crave the affections of these fatherly figures.

My life carried with it a certain unsavoury reputation. And as we drove to the conference, I heard something I didn't really want to hear.

'One of the gossips at church has been telling people about your past,' my boyfriend told me.

'Yeah, I know exactly what she would be saying,' I replied.

'But that's your past – don't worry about it,' he said. Yet I remember being angry and embarrassed about it. And my heart sank at the thought of others talking about my abortions.

We arrived late and the conference had already begun. I was totally overwhelmed at the thousands of people packed into the hall. Not so long before, I'd been convinced that Christians either got together in vicars' living rooms for tea and cakes, or as gangs of fanatical Bible bashers accosting unwary Saturday shoppers. The conference was different; the air was thick with what I can only describe as the presence of God. Obviously I could not literally see God, but it felt like the thousands of people were enveloped in a cloud of electricity. No sooner had we arrived than an invitation was announced. It was for people to approach the stage if they wanted to give their lives to Jesus. I didn't even know what that meant – but my heart began to pound. I had to check that it was not about to burst from my chest. I was lifted off my seat and found myself walking forwards. It felt as if I was acting against my will, but even as I questioned what on earth I was doing, my arms and legs kept moving.

As I walked to the front, I had to pass one of the gossips. Immediately, I was plunged into feelings of inadequacy and guilt. She knew about my abortions, and yet I was walking forwards for forgiveness. I then saw the Elim worship leader at the front of the stage. The doubts continued. Surely in his eyes I wasn't qualified to be doing this. He knew I had only been at church for a few weeks. How could I present myself before God like this? What a delusion, to think that God had really called me to live for him!

The attacks became more vicious, and everything inside me tried to resist approaching the stage. But I felt like two invisible beings had literally taken my arms and were carrying me to the front. I was trying to physically stop myself from walking because I felt so terrible and worthless. *What power is this?* I thought. *Is it God?* I certainly wasn't projecting it. Every step became a battle. The gossip was looking at me. What would she think? She knows who I am, what I'm like, and what I've done. She wouldn't want me to go forwards. The man at the front, what would he think? He knows I'm not qualified to understand what I'm doing. He wouldn't want me to take another step. Should I turn back for their sake and not make a fool of myself?

When I reached the front, I remembered that I had asked God if there was anything that he wanted me to do for him. This was his answer. He wanted me to get right with him, to make a commitment and let him enter into my life for good. He wanted me to do this so much, that he had practically lifted me up and carried me towards him. I was asked to repeat a prayer of forgiveness in recognition of what Jesus had done for me on the cross – taken all the punishment for the bad things I'd done. Having felt the change since wanting to end my life, and having read about Jesus' compassion for lost and broken people such as me, I was prepared to make the commitment. People prayed for me. They prayed a strange prayer for God's Spirit, the Holy Spirit, to descend on me. I felt the most amazing torrent of love and peace wash through me again. I turned around to see a man standing directly behind me. He pressed a piece of paper into my hand and squeezed it tight.

'This is for you,' he said. 'It is for no one else here, just for you.'

On the paper were written the words:

> You are doing the right thing stepping out for him. He will mightily bless you for it, and you will bring many people to his kingdom.

That message was the total opposite of what I had often been told in my past. Up to that point, I had believed that I was useless. These words, although Christian in their language and tone, instantly dismissed the doubts and attacks I had faced. It no longer mattered what anyone might be thinking or what I thought of myself. I knew this force was from God, I knew he was real. I knew that he was bigger than me. Despite the noise of my world that had shut him out, God knew my deepest needs and had listened to my most secret prayers and desires. Even the ones that I didn't think he could hear.

What I learned that day was that Jesus accepts and forgives those who cry out their need for him. At my most weak and pathetic, written off and abandoned by the world, I had called to him. I had not earned his attention or studied to gain a certificate of his approval. It was easier to think that I had to tidy myself up before God would accept me, but God accepted me in the heart of my mess and shame. I had committed my life to him, and I believed that he was equally committed to sorting that mess out.

We drove back to Jenny Quaif's house. She was going away on holiday and I was due to look after her house as a favour. That night I could only lie on my bed and think about the words on the piece of paper. I slept for about an hour. When I had gone out with a new boyfriend for the first time, I would think about them all night, excitedly running through the details of our meeting in my head. This was a similar feeling, but so much more intense. It was rooted in the supernatural, outside the realms of anything I had experienced. Naturally, I worried about the honeymoon period, because I knew that I ran on extremes. I took drugs to cope with such extremes. They had seen me through the fallout of broken relationships. But the real drug was in the power of escapism the relationships had offered me.

This time, rather than allowing me to escape, God was about to transform my existing world. The words on the paper said that I had 'stepped out' for him, and that he would 'mightily bless me' for choosing this. What did they mean? What did it mean to 'bring many people to his kingdom'? All I knew was that my life had changed because I had made a decision to follow Jesus. I clutched the paper and let the words sink deep into my heart. I didn't want to let this go because I feared being left alone again.

The following morning I saw Jenny in the kitchen before she left for her holiday.

'I hardly slept last night,' I told her. 'I am still buzzing with it all – even now. The man who gave me that note could never have known how much it would mean to me.'

'What wonderful news,' Jenny responded with a big smile. 'God clearly has big plans for you.'

Jenny was shy and rarely gave her emotions away. But now, tears streamed down her face. It was shocking to see other people reacting so positively to my life. I felt a sense of being loved, not only by Jesus, but by people as well. On the following Sunday I was asked to stand in front of the church and tell everyone what had happened. The support was amazing. Suddenly, I knew I was accepted.

10

The Presence

I was so in love with God. And it was obvious to everyone around me. People would say, 'Here comes smiley
Amanda.' I just couldn't stop smiling. So when Andy
came round to visit Danielle, I told him about my going
to church, reading the Bible and becoming a Christian. I
declared naively that now I had found God, there would
be no more pain in my life.

Andy's reaction wasn't as negative as I had expected.
He complained and questioned why I would want to
read about God. In his opinion, he had heard it all
before. In prison he had seen inmates pretend to become
Christians to receive shorter sentences. His answer was,
'Whatever makes you happy.' I thought about that; the
self-centered pursuit of whatever made me happy had
caused most of my problems in the first place!

I tried talking to Andy about God. I was over-zealous.
But I knew that if it hadn't been for God's own zealous
intervention in my life, I might not have been around to
talk to anyone. God had stepped in to save me, and so I
spoke to people with the enthusiasm of somebody who
had literally been saved. I wasn't about to keep it a
secret. When I became a Christian, I remember looking

at Andy and loving him so much that it worried me. We might not have been married, but we had created a child together, and I was confused over the implications of what this situation meant to God. I was afraid that he would want me to go back to Andy. After all, I had given God more than my Sunday mornings. I had given him my life, which included my daughter and my relationships.

As soon as I had made the commitment to become a Christian, I wanted to run around and tell everybody. I phoned my sister Carol and shared my experiences with her. Carol had recently been to see a spiritualist about Mum. The medium she visited told Carol that she could see Mum sitting next to her. Carol wanted me to be the first to hear this news. In my new-found passion for Jesus Christ, I questioned her visit, knowing that spiritualism wasn't compatible with being a Christian. But assuming that I was trying to correct her life, she told me off for daring to preach to her. My other sisters saw my 'conversion' as a mere phase which, like my relationships, would fizzle out as soon as I found something more appealing to cling on to.

I was still in a relationship with my boyfriend from church, but it wasn't working. He had been brought up as a Christian, whereas I had stumbled into it like falling over a stack of suitcases, spilling luggage everywhere. We found it difficult relating to each other's past experiences, but he did accompany me on my early Christian walk. Together, we drove along the south coast to Littlehampton, to an event called 'Cutting Edge'. Young people from all over the country would just swarm to this new event. There was a feeling of real freedom in expressing our love for God. People spoke passionately about having a purpose, and that there was no mistake that God had called them. I had never heard people speak with such assurance. Did God have a purpose and a plan for me? I had once been called Mum's biggest mistake, but now I wanted to find out just what God's plan was for his broken little daughter.

The dancers at the event were fantastic, especially one girl in particular – Anna. She danced like a gymnast, with flags. As she moved, her face shone, impressing me far more than her obvious technique and ability. It was a powerful inspiration to see her dance not for attention or applause, but for God. She was dancing for her Father. I looked at the dancer, and desired the same freedom of expression for myself. As I recommitted my heart to dancing, I felt an overwhelming assurance that it was something God wanted me to do. I set out to acquire some flags of my own!

When I returned to church every fibre of my body buzzed and tingled as I was urged to dance. I found out that it is impossible to ignore the immediacy of God when he encourages and inspires – this is how I learned that it was God's voice physically leading me into action. I discovered that I still have a choice, and it is both exciting and fearful, but it is faith that overrides the fear. God's voice can be a sense, an instinct, a feeling or clear knowledge; sometimes even an audible whisper. I also discovered that although he speaks to us as individuals, his voice will never contradict the Bible. Whereas before I had cowered in the dark, God was opening my spirit to his voice. As I learned to talk to my new Father, I also learned to listen to him. My prayers were never directed internally; God was not my 'inner self', he was an external loving Creator, and through faith in him he led me back into dancing.

At church, when I felt my heart hammer against my chest, God would urge me, 'Go to the front', and so I danced whether I felt good or bad. I began to dance and wind my way towards the front of the church. I still felt worthless on the inside, but when I danced I became like a snake shedding its skin. Every time I shed a layer of old skin, I was able to grow again. Soon I felt old beliefs being cast off, all my wrong beliefs about the world and myself. Dancing for God allowed me to express my longing for him, and allowed him to cast off my fear of people – this fear had held me captive all my life. I was troubled when a lady at church made a point of telling me that this 'honeymoon' period would end; I feared this because my dealings with such moments had always been disastrous.

Despite my new faith, I continued my relationship with old friends. Their reaction to my attempted new path was to laugh and roll a joint. My response was to sit and smoke it with them. I felt terrible because it no longer felt right. As soon as I fed my mind with drugs I found myself without God's accompanying peace. When I first started seeing my church boyfriend, I had given up smoking. It had happened suddenly, free from withdrawal symptoms and cravings. I made a point of telling Andy that my old ways were over. But when I saw my friends who still inhabited the world of addiction, I fell back into habits that dismayed me.

One day, a couple of guys from church, Augie and Tim, paid me a visit.

'This is Tim,' said Augie, 'he's got an amazing story!'

I had seen Tim before, as he had started coming along to church about the same time as me. But I had never heard his story.

'I was a heroin addict,' Tim told me, 'and overnight God took away that addiction.'

'Wow – that is incredible!' I said. 'I have friends who are heroin addicts and have struggled to come off it – even through rehab.'

Tim had experienced the same peace I had, by crying out from his own bed of misery. The reality of his testimony was that God could take addictions away – permanently.

Smoking dope amplified my mood swings, from depression and lethargy to manic excitement and paranoia. I felt ashamed that I could not stick to my word. One minute I would be high on God; the next minute I would be rolling a joint. I just felt awful, because I felt I was letting God down.

This continued over the next few weeks; I was living free from cravings only for them to reclaim their former hold. I fell on my knees in front of God, asking for his help. It was a long battle, but I stuck with God and his church. I never stopped asking him to speak to me, and he never stopped answering. God would either show me my true value in his eyes, which would instantly melt my heart, or he would convict me about something that he wanted to deal with. I didn't want to hear him mention the smoking though! That fight was too difficult. I secretly hoped that God would overlook it. But the addiction had been imprinted on me since primary school, and I knew that when I touched nicotine, dope followed. There were times when I would even attend church stoned. I hated that. But despite the baggage that I had carried into this new phase of life, I still wanted to declare my faith publicly. So the next step was to be baptised.

I had already seen this happen in the Elim church. People would tell their life story and how they had found their faith. Then they would be 'dunked' underwater in a tank of water – or even in the sea. It's not a new fad. The practice dates all the way back to the historical beginnings of Christianity.

I had given my life to God. I believed that Jesus was the way. I wanted to follow this man who dealt with people with love and compassion. Even Jesus himself was baptised, and he asked his followers to do the same. For us, it becomes a symbolic washing away of our old lives – as we emerge from the water renewed.

Our church's baptisms were being held in the sea, and there were nine people telling their stories. Then it was my turn. I was already an emotional wreck listening to the other new Christians tell their stories. When I had to tell mine, I could hardly speak through my tears. A lady prayed for me, saying that I had not seen anything yet regarding what God was going to do for me. When I walked into the sea, I remembered God's public approval of Jesus as he was baptised in the River Jordan. Despite the mess I was in, and despite the fact that I had never persevered or succeeded at anything, God put his seal of approval on me for accepting his Son. In doing so, he publicly washed the record of my past life clean.

I soon began to discover that Christians could not live on spiritual highs alone. After Jesus was baptised, and experienced God's blessing, he wandered alone into the desert. Here he was attacked, tested, refined and strengthened. I struggled with Christians who claimed to have a dynamic relationship with the living God, only to criticise and condemn anyone who dared approach their defences. It occurred to me that people can hide from God in religion, and I wanted to shake the dead religion out of people. I wanted to shine for God, to accept all the healing and blessings that he had stored up for me and reflect his love for the world. However, God's journey is not a constant walk of spectacular mountain peaks. I experienced this for myself when, having been baptised, I found myself sliding back down a slippery slope towards my old ways.

It was suggested that I move in with a Christian girl. I thought that to say no would be unwise. But it was the wrong decision; a disaster from the beginning.

My new housemate chain-smoked, which didn't help my problem, and so my battle with addiction continued. After splitting up with my church boyfriend, I started seeing another guy who worked in a burger bar across the road. I hoped that he would also become a Christian, once he saw the difference that faith had made to my life. I found his negative response to my faith unbelievable; I assumed that everybody wanted to be loved by a perfect Father.

Most of my Christian friends, who were new to this walk themselves, had rekindled old habits. However, I made sure that throughout my own difficulties I did not stray from church and Christian community. I read God's Word and was moved by his son Jesus. I attended church, cried, sang and danced my heart out, and through all of this, I heard God's voice. I felt terrible for letting God down, especially after all he had promised me. I hated the fact that I was grieving him. My old friends accused me of being a hypocrite for attending church, but I knew that God loved me as I was. He might have hated my continuing addiction, but he wanted me at church.

Unfortunately, once I had fallen back into old habits, trying to fight my way out was like climbing a wall coated with oil. I could not gain a foothold. As my new boyfriend and I started sleeping together, I allowed spiritual ground to be taken back from God. I even justified it, convincing myself that I would bring my boyfriend to God, but I knew our relationship had to end.

Where most men still wouldn't go near me because of Andy's violent reputation, my new boyfriend didn't mind. He was kind, gentle, and great with Danielle. Ironically, he represented everything I had looked for before I had met God. However, whereas my boyfriend may have been a fulfilment of past fantasies, I recognised that such a relationship, however safe, was not the answer. I reflected on my former relationship with Andy, realising that his attitude towards me had never been one of pure evil, nor had our quarrels ever been one-sided. I had been damaged long before I met Andy – first blaming the world for my pain and then lashing out at the people around me. Being with my new boyfriend may have come as a refreshing break from previous failures, but God wanted to save me from my own abused emotions. The temptation to view my new relationship as the answer was strong. However, I knew that my Saviour was Christ. Without him, I could only live a cycle of unfulfilled dreams.

Throughout these attacking doubts, I was still able to read the Bible, and I learned to speak to God in prayer. While receiving prayer in church, I sometimes heard people speaking in other languages. The Bible describes this as 'speaking in tongues', and it is referred to as a gift of the Spirit. I had read about this but did not think that it was meant for me. However, one day, while somebody was praying for me, I felt a warm sensation wash through me. I received two words that, while unintelligible, became words of extreme importance. For about a week I could not forget them, and so one day while walking along the road, I said to God that I was bored of thinking about these strange words, and that I wanted some more.

I felt an overwhelming presence within me and I uttered words that I could not understand but that brought with them a tremendous sense of freedom. The following Sunday at church I felt my heart race as during the service I knew that I had to speak in tongues. As I was considering this, wondering whether I was in fact going crazy, the pastor said that he believed somebody had a message for the church in tongues, and encouraged whoever it was not to hold back. I spoke out the strange words, and as I did I felt a foot taller. Somebody else in the congregation said that they had the interpretation, and as they gave the church the meaning of what had been said, their very words described perfectly how I was feeling.

Jesus says that God is our Father, and so I began to address him as one. This was easy because I had no father to compare him to. I thanked God that something real had happened. He was a tangible presence, beyond any self-willed New Age energy I may have projected. I began to read through the account of the crucifixion, of how Jesus chose his execution as an act of sacrifice and obedience. I realised that God had already done so much for me, and so I asked him to tell me of anything I could do for him.

God had become more than a belief, he had become my fulfilment. I had a personal relationship that needed his presence. My dependence on God was not a delusion; the delusion was found in my independence from God and dependence on myself. I liked my boyfriend, but neither planned nor wanted the sexual relationship. I tried to say no, but I was already too entrenched in my old ways to stop myself. Once again, I was sleeping with someone because it was what I knew, and I was getting stoned to numb the conflict. My life seemed a million miles away from my heartfelt convictions that I would live for God. I hated myself for going to church to sing and worship, only to then live another unfaithful week. There were two roads before me and I was currently walking between them.

I lay on my bed, the place where I first met with God. Sensing the open jaws of failure around me, I cried out to him that I hated myself. I recommitted myself to him, declaring that I wanted to walk his road. As I did this, I saw a picture in my mind. It was of a fireplace, and walking towards the fire with her hand poised to grab the flames was a little toddler – Danielle.

I heard her scream as the flames burned her hand and she pulled away in agony. The picture and accompanying emotions were vivid. I wanted to step in and save the girl from further pain.

A voice said to me, 'What would you do with that little girl?'

'I'd grab hold of that little girl and I'd run to the freezer and I'd pack her hand in ice and I would not let her go until the pain had gone.'

The voice continued, 'That is how I feel about you. Now what would you do with the fireplace?'

I looked at the fireplace. 'I'd go out and I'd buy a fireguard and I'd make sure it never happened again.'

'Yes, and that fireguard is the Holy Spirit, who protects you from what harms you. I know you are hurting, but trust me, as toddlers grow out of each phase, you will grow out of this.'

The picture disappeared.

11

Broken Pot

'I can't give up dope,' I said. My bleak admission came out on a sunny day, while sitting on the beach. I had a new friend with me, a counsellor called Christine Beales. I told her about my nicotine and cannabis addictions, and claimed I could not stop. Christine said that I had done it once before, so I could do it again. She neither pampered me nor pandered to my self-pity.

Christine had been recommended by the Elim pastor. This man had real insight into what it was like to be fatherless, as his father had walked out on him as a child. He was a great help to me when I told him and his wife about how I was still addicted to smoking dope – and how I was engaged in a sexual relationship that I could not leave. I told them that I believed the reason was because I had been raped when I was a young girl. It was the first time since the age of thirteen that I had thought about that incident. The pastor replied that if it was true that I had been abused, then the cycle needed to be broken.

The next concern was my relationship with my boyfriend. It was wrong because it was hurting me. Alone, on the kitchen floor, I pleaded to God, 'God, if this relationship is not what you want, then I am so sorry, please take it away.'

The next day I received a phone call from my boyfriend. In a polite but firm tone, he ended the relationship. Instead of the searing pain of rejection, I felt the warmth and acceptance of God. I celebrated his answer to my prayers.

I moved out of home and into my friend Callie's house for a couple of weeks. By this time the relationship between Andy and I was really breaking down. We had made an unwelcome return to familiar days when he would either be pleasant or he would play the prison psychopath. When I dropped Danielle off or returned to collect her, I never knew what to expect from him. When Andy chased me down the street and pressed his fist into my face with a fresh volley of threats, I would pray, 'Jesus help me!' because I didn't know who was in control.

He threatened to take Danielle away from me. Although our relationship was over, our two worlds continued to collide violently in front of Danielle. It broke my heart when she cried out for us to stop in the middle of one such argument. At the age of three, she was witnessing the violence that I had always strived to protect her from.

The conflict between us reached a destructive climax. Andy lost his temper and refused to give Danielle back. I prayed about going to the police, knowing that their involvement would be counted as the lowest form of treachery. Where I came from, you did not 'grass' on a mate. Having explained the situation to the authorities, they escorted me to Andy's house to reclaim my daughter. It was a cold transaction but something that had to be done. The police drove me home to Callie's, and on the way one of the policemen told me that he had felt sorry for Andy. I remembered how Andy had looked at me in horror as they took Danielle away from him. He could not understand why I had involved the police.

Callie suggested that I needed to remove myself from the confrontation altogether. An arrangement was made in which she delivered Danielle like a parcel to Andy, and then Andy's father would return her home safely. It successfully cut me out of the picture, freeing me from having to face Andy's abusive temper. For a couple of months I had no contact with him at all. I was happier, and Danielle was happier because her visits to her father were free from arguing parents.

During this time at Callie's, away from my old life, I managed to stop smoking dope. I asked God to take away the cravings. And he did. One morning I woke up, and the old feelings had gone. I had smoked cigarettes since primary school, so it was a huge part of me. It brought tremendous freedom when that craving left – and the closeness with God came flooding back.

Suddenly I began to hate the smell of cigarettes on my clothes, in my hair, in my house and on Danielle. Drawing smoke into my lungs to blow it out again seemed futile and weak. God didn't issue a strict 'thou shalt not', but instead highlighted the stink of what I was inhaling, and my lack of control in letting drugs influence my mind. He took away the craving and broke the addiction. I was back on the path, walking by his side, instead of using my energy to run in the opposite direction.

From my friend Callie's house, I moved on with Danielle to live with Christine Beales and I loved being part of her family. There was so much laughter around the kitchen table, which was something I had never known – I'd known only lies and violence. Christine gave me the advice of a mother and, because of her relationship with

God, her advice was born from spiritual discipline. She prayed with me and for me, which was fantastic; she became my spiritual mother. Christine wasn't my saviour, Jesus was, and she wasn't about to solve all my problems. But she was one of the first people who really believed in me and accepted me unconditionally.

I learned that we all fall short of God's standards. Smoking dope had been a very external problem. I remember how other Christians had looked down their noses at me, but their judgement was as wrong as my addiction. I knew this because God is the judge, and he reads our hearts. My heart was longing to do the right thing for him, even if I struggled to achieve it in practice. Through Christine, I learned to look to God for my strength and wisdom, and I began to experience a deeper understanding of my faith beyond simply attending church once a week.

Throughout this time I had been praying for a husband, and it was more than just the occasional prayer. One of my fears was that I would be left alone. With the help of my friends Tim, Augie and his wife Sam, we all prayed that if it was God's desire for me to be married, then he would help me to find the right person.

We travelled to a weekend conference in Prestatyn in Wales. During the very first meeting, a man said, 'God wants you to stop fretting and worrying about a husband, because he has got somebody in mind for you, and he is wonderful.'

I remember the word 'wonderful' being very poignant. As the stranger said this, Tim walked past. I thought, *Is he talking about Tim?* However, I had been told to stop fretting and so I left it alone. From that day, I felt peace about the situation. I knew now that I would meet somebody and that he was going to be right for me.

Based on my previous experience with relationships, this was going to take a miracle.

There was a speaker at the conference talking about the biblical theme of the potter and the clay. I listened to him describe how a skilled potter can mould the clay into any shape he wants. He said that God is like the potter and we are like the clay. Sometimes a potter will take an old broken pot, break it down into clay again, and then rebuild it to make something beautiful. This is a good picture of what God does with us; he breaks us down, only to rebuild us. Then, just as a potter will pour water into a new pot, God will pour his life into us, and it will overflow. One pot can hold enough water to quench the thirst of many people; so God's life will pour out of us for the benefit of others.

The speaker then illustrated how the potter smoothes out all the edges of the pot, and carefully examines its surface for cracks and air holes. If they remain, then as soon as the pot is placed in the heat of the kiln, it will crack and become useless. It was a powerful reminder of the words I received when I gave my life to Jesus – how he would mightily bless me to bring others to his kingdom. I had been raring to go, telling God, 'Come on then! What are you waiting for?' I had told people about God, standing as a witness to the changes he had brought to my life. So far not a lot had happened. I felt like a constant disappointment, especially within my own family. Now I was able to say to God, 'You are the potter, I am the clay. You are in charge, not me.'

I sensed that he needed to mend the broken pot.

12

Fresh Visions

I had some frightening questions as a young believer. Christian teaching now told me that no one can come to God except through Jesus. I had no personal evidence that my mum had made her peace with him during her lifetime. So where did that leave her?

I didn't know whether I should be asking God about Mum. I knew that God is not to be used as a medium. Tarot cards, horoscopes, Ouija boards, spells – God warns us to stay away from all such spiritual dabbling. However, I asked him directly because I wanted to know where she was. Although I had the faith to pray about it, I didn't expect him to answer.

While looking after Jenny's children, I watched another video, but this one was about a man called Ian McCormack. Ian lived a life of surfing and drugs. He was stung one night by several box jellyfish while diving, off the island of Mauritius. They are also known as the Portuguese Man-of-War and their venom is fatal. Ian was an atheist, but while dying on the way to hospital, he saw a vision of his mother praying for him. As he watched his life flash before his eyes, Ian called out to God before he died. He found himself in a place of isolation and terror.

There was no light, only total darkness. He could not feel his body, but he knew the experience was real. Every time he tried to cry out, he heard cruel and evil voices telling him to 'Shut up!' because he deserved to be there. If there was a God then he wasn't present, and Ian described this place as hell. It was a complete and terrifying separation from the presence of God.

Ian then appeared before God and he was shown heaven. He asked for forgiveness for every selfish thing he had ever done in his life, a life spent living for nothing but his own pleasure. As he spoke with God, Ian experienced waves of overwhelming love and acceptance. Whereas I had lain on my bed in darkness, Ian had physically stood before God to receive his salvation. The love was the same; it is there for everybody who approaches Jesus in true and humble belief and repentance.

Ian was given a choice whether to stay in heaven or return to earth. He asked God if he could stay, because there was nothing left for him on earth. But he then realised that if he didn't return, his mother would not know what had happened to her son. He woke up in the hospital to the distressed faces of the doctors; they had hung a tag from Ian's toe having already pronounced him dead. It was an incredible story and it made me think of Mum.

What if God had fought for her even during her last dying hours on earth? What if Mum had turned towards the face of Jesus and stretched out her hand for his? If she had then I certainly didn't know, but Jesus knew and so I asked him, 'Where is my mum? Has she gone with you?'

That very second, I had a vision of Mum standing before God. She asked him to forgive her, and he said 'Yes', because her words were enough. Then he told her that he was going to use Mandy to bring the rest of the family to him. The vision was as real as the girl burning her hand in the flames; God had once again answered my prayers of faith.

It was such a perfect vision of Mum that I immediately began to wonder whether it was really a triumph of my imagination. I knew that salvation could only happen before death, not afterwards. Had my mum, then, turned to Jesus even as she lay dying? Had God really said these things to me? Does he honestly allow such privileged information to pass from heaven to earth? The attacks crept in as Satan's whispers targeted God's truth. A few weeks later, I felt a strong urge to visit Jenny Quaif. As I sat on her sofa, she confessed it being strange that I should visit because that very morning she had woken with a vision of my mum. I was defensive because Jenny had never met Mum. I had already heard all the negative opinions possible regarding Mum and I was cautious as to what Jenny had to say.

Jenny told me that she had seen a vision of my mum standing before God. It was the same vision I had seen myself, with the same words, and because Jenny had never known me as 'Mandy', it was all the more potent. It was God's confirmation that before Mum had died she had been saved. I cried in front of Jenny, 'Why has God told me all of this?' I was in awe of his sharing of heaven's secrets; it was enough just to feel his presence, how could I be worth this? Again, I asked why and Jenny simply said, 'It's because he loves you.'

God had revealed to me that Mum had asked him to forgive her as she was dying. She was in his kingdom of heaven. Her mind and opinions had been recreated, just like mine had because of the Holy Spirit here on earth. I realised that if Mum were here today, forgiven from sinful rebellion and saved from spiritual death, then she would say sorry for everything she had spoken over my life. God was healing my severed relationship with Mum, and this was a powerful beginning.

My friendship increased with Tim, Augie and Sam, and with their help I continued to pray for a husband. They were my first close friends at the church, and we spent a lot of time growing, praying and worshipping as young Christians. Tim and Augie were not the kind of men who habitually twisted everything into sexual innuendo and casual smut; I knew that I could trust them. We loved God, and their conviction helped to inspire me when I was tempted back into old ways. Augie refused to touch alcohol, knowing that his weakness was in drinking, and Tim's overnight rescue from heroin addiction was amazing. It was unheard of among all the addicts I had known. We had all met God in intense conversions, and we believed every word of God's Bible. Augie inspired us to talk to the Saturday shoppers in Worthing town centre. We were passionate and sensitive in sharing our testimonies. A few people began to search for God themselves on the strength of what he had already done for us.

One evening I was lying on Augie's sofa praying for a husband. I sensed a voice say to me, 'Stop praying because you will be married within a year.'

I leapt up and down, jumping around the room. Could this really be true? Would I find the relationship that I had longed for? I told Augie and he said sensibly that I should test these things by asking God for confirmation, but I shrugged it off. This was real; I knew it was God because I had felt something happen; it was like a chain breaking from me.

A couple of months later, I began to look at Tim differently. I shook it off in disbelief but these emerging feelings for Tim lingered. He was living with a couple of our friends, so I saw him more than ever, but I struggled with seeing him as anything more than just a good friend.

Tim wanted to travel the world and evangelise. The last thing he intended to do was get married. He was a man who was unashamed of his faith, and I was attracted to this passion. We had both come to church within a couple of weeks of one another. We had grown together, and I was also developing a friendship with Tim's mum, Jen.

I first met Jen and Tim's father Bernard at church. They were not Christians and had come to see Tim's baptism. Tim had only been a Christian for a couple of weeks. He was so overwhelmed by what God had done for him, he joined a church and was baptised almost immediately. Jen had recently been diagnosed with cancer, and had been told that she had about six months to live. When she learned this, the doctor left the room, but a female nurse stayed to comfort them, and both Jen and Bernard were touched by her compassion and support. They were surprised when they saw the same nurse singing on the church stage the morning they had come to see their son get baptised.

'What did you think of the service, then?' a church member asked Bernard.

'I've never seen such a load of rubbish in all my life,' he fired back. Then he stormed out of the building.

Jen wanted to return to church and Bernard wanted to support her. He struggled, sometimes fuming as he marched out of church in his battle against God. His wife was terminally ill, and his youngest son was preaching about God's love. But as time progressed, he began to look forward to church, even admitting that he needed it. God is patient and never gives up, and once he has called our name, there is nowhere left to hide, no matter how fast or far we run.

Jen wanted to know God, and saw herself as a good person. Tim told her that in order to be accepted by God she needed to believe in Jesus and repent of her sins. This is something the world despises having to hear. Jen couldn't see how she had sinned and didn't know what to repent of. What we understand as sin is a world apart from what God understands. Our sin is not only found in the crimes that society locks up in its prisons, but in every living person. We sin in every thought and act that we have separated from God. Our rejection of God is the crime that the human race needs to repent of. A lot of people like me, Tim, Ian McCormack, and Jen with her cancer, are taken to the last hurdle before we give up our fight, but God calls to us all, every single day.

Tim and Augie prayed that God would show Jen that even as a good person, she had still been in the wrong place with God, living independently from him. They prayed for hours until four in the morning, when suddenly they felt it right to stop. The following day Tim visited his mum and she said to him, 'You won't believe what happened to me last night. I was woken up at four o'clock in the morning, and all of a sudden every selfish thought and every selfish act that I had ever committed was shown to me. Even when I thought I was doing right, I had been acting against God, and I told him how sorry I was for all of it.'

It was an amazing experience for both Tim and his mum.

Tim took me out for coffee one day, and practically interviewed me about what I thought about his future plans to travel. I laughed because he knew my answers already, but it was Tim's nature to be as methodical as possible. He wanted it all worked out before risking any emotional investment. A couple of weeks later I visited the house where Tim was staying. We watched a film together and he put his arm around me. These first delicate and tentative moments brought us closer together. We both understood that because of our faith, any commitment to a relationship would lead to marriage.

After about a month of going out together, Tim had to go away for a weekend. Before he left we decided to pray, asking God that if it was right for us to get married, then could he please make it clear. Tim left and I spent the weekend at home. As I was looking through my diary, I flipped to 14 September and noticed that somebody had written in highlighted pen 'my wedding day'. I laughed because I hadn't written it. When Tim returned, I went to see him and he had his yearly planner unfolded across his bedroom floor. I walked in and pointed to the same date, announcing to Tim that it was going to be our wedding day.

Tim wasn't surprised by my assurance. Moments before I had arrived, he had also seen the very same words, written in the same pen, circling the same date, 14 September. We believed that God had deliberately chosen to confirm this so blatantly. We hardly trusted our own emotions because we were both damaged from previous relationships. We needed God to literally highlight his desired plan, to speak to us clearly, because we could only trust something as important as marriage to God alone.

Strange things happen when you ask God to direct your life.

13

Healing Stream

The wedding plans were going ahead. The date had been set for 14 September. Meanwhile, Tim and I decided to return to the annual conference. On the way there Tim sat in the front of the car chatting with a friend, while I sat in the back staring at the world through the window. I had stared out of windows before, but the circumstances had been very different. I am not going to pretend to understand God's timing, but all of a sudden, in the back of the car, I saw the entire scene of myself being raped when I was thirteen. It was as vivid as sitting down and watching a film.

Not only did I see it with my eyes, but I also felt every terrifying emotional detail of the rape. Although I could see myself trying to fight the boys off, I could also hear Mum speaking to me when I was four. I heard her say how men are to be used and we are no different. The rape became the living reality of her disposable attitude towards sex. Her very words were staring me in the face, bearing down with all their catastrophic weight. I walked away from Michelle's house having been raped by her brothers. I heard her words that had tormented and reduced me to nothing: 'What's the matter? Aren't my brothers good enough for you?' It was one stab in the heart after another as I told myself, 'It doesn't matter. Tomorrow's another day. Forget it. Get over it. Move on!' Had I really said those things? Had I really applied so little worth to my life?

This all took place simultaneously, but it wasn't confusing. God is not a God of confusion, but of clarity and truth. He showed me the poison of the words spoken over me: Mum's teaching manifesting in the belief that, having been raped, I could tell myself it was just another day. I took on board not only Mum's words, but Michelle's too.

I remember watching the news or television dramas where people had been raped. They would be so angry, feeling violated and dirty, but I could not put myself in that place. While watching this sickening rerun and listening to Mum's verbal soundtrack, what hurt the most was that I had never allowed myself to be angry. I had never felt that I had been wronged, and never believed that I was worth more. From the back of the car I asked bitter questions. 'Oh, Mum, *why* did you teach me to feel that low about myself, to lack any confidence and self-esteem? *Why* did you teach me such a throw-away attitude towards myself, my body and towards sex?' I could not believe that I had turned my back, thinking it would have such little consequence in my life.

In that one instant during our car journey, I could see how the rape had affected me. Even as a Christian I struggled with the fear of rejection, wanting to back out of relationships as soon as things became too real, too physical, too close for comfort. Had God triggered this because I was about to get married? I had asked him to deal with things quickly, and I was about to enter the spiritual bond of marriage. I already feared being trapped.

This was the avalanche. This was the oncoming land-slide of emotion that God had prepared long ago, but it wasn't a disaster. God's avalanche had not crashed down in the back seat of the car to wreak havoc and destruction. He was clearing the way to reveal his new living landscape that had been buried underneath.

I had to look at my life through God's eyes, to face my wounds with him. When I first arrived at church, week after week I would stand at the front to grab hold of any prayer I could get. I had been a spiritual orphan, des-perate and starving. The pastor once told me, 'Ask God to show you how he sees you.'

I didn't understand. I had tried to accept the value that people said God had placed upon me, but it had been difficult. Now God had revealed the existence of a dark room. It was his desire to open the door and walk me through this room. I had ignored the possibility of any such place, pretending that the pain and damage didn't exist. Now it was time to enter that room with Jesus, to see what he had always known.

I saw what had been there to start with: the beaten-down furniture and mouldy walls, the filthy floor and dirty ceilings. It was dark and ugly, but I had to look because this was where I had hidden all my pain. It could not be ignored any longer, not if I wanted to move on with both God and a husband. For the time being, all I could do was gaze at it, as it brought back emotions of anger, resentment and fear.

We arrived at the conference and Tim asked if I was OK. I told him that God had just shown me something and I needed to talk to him later. We put some time aside for each other, and I told him everything that God had told me about the rape and its consequences. Tim was the first person I had told in detail, and it was the first time I had ever cried about it. We prayed, giving this new and unfamiliar landscape wholeheartedly to God. But we were both upset and so we took it no further for the duration of the conference. When I returned home, I spoke to Christine Beales about the events in the car. Until now, I thought smoking had been my biggest problem, so I asked her, 'Do you think I might need some prayer for this?'

Her answer was a resounding 'Yes!' and being a counsellor, she knew exactly what to do. We began to pray together. Tim was asked if he wanted to join us and although he said 'Yes', I didn't want him there because in some ways he was more upset than I was. Looking into this dark room caused me to struggle with our relationship, and Tim had been pushed away in the process. God showed me the mechanisms of his healing, and it was like staring into the sun to then be branded by its after-image, such was the potency of God's work. Every time I was reminded of the rape, it was as though it had taken place only a split second before.

As God walked me through my healing, I could not accept any affection from Tim. Christine explained to him how I was feeling, and he was very patient. She voiced concern over the fact that we were due to be married in around six weeks' time, and asked me whether I wanted to call it off. However, 14 September was God's exclusive date, and so I remained convinced that God would complete what he needed to do before my wedding day. He was the potter and I was the clay.

I remembered asking God to break me in order to heal me. The prayer and chats with Christine began to free my capacity to cry and mourn. She said that I had to first forgive the two brothers, and despite feeling angry, I found I could do this. It was much harder to forgive their sister Michelle, but I had to keep giving it back to God. I could not afford to hold onto any of this pain, and

I struggled because of the degrading feelings that surfaced. Their personal forgiveness was between them and God, but I had to forgive them for the harm they had inflicted on me. I learned that judgement of this world is reserved for God alone. No matter how much I have been mistreated, God has not given me any right to judge. My pain and injustice have to be given to Jesus, over and over again. In holding on to it, I damage others and myself. Ultimately, I damage my relationship with God.

The hardest part of the healing process was in forgiving Mum. God reminded me that she had asked him for forgiveness before she died, so I knew it was possible. As much as I saw myself as being very different to Mum, I had already begun to devalue men and sex. I had to forgive her. Without God's intervention in my life, I imagined that Mum's beliefs would have become mine, and Danielle would one day have to forgive me. Despite meditating on Mum's repentance, I was sad that she never told me about my father, sad over what she taught me about sex, and sad that she never really confessed to loving me. She did once say, 'I love you, but I don't like you.' But that's not the same as expressing wholehearted love, is it?

While praying I saw a picture of a stream filled with God's living water. The water was flowing fast and it carried a fallen tree, which had jammed itself across the stream. While the water continued to flow around and sometimes over the obstacle, it was catching bits of moss and twigs. God revealed to me that this decaying chunk of dead wood represented Mum's early teaching. When my uncle touched me, the incident had become wedged on Mum's perspective of sex. When Mary and her husband frightened me, the log had gathered many broken twigs; I told myself it was OK, because I was used to being fondled and groped by people. By the time I was raped by the two brothers, I no longer saw it as abuse. It was just something that people did to me. I was incapable of pushing past Mum's perspective; I could not get through to the freedom that lay downstream.

My absent father and Mum's absent love had created a void. In that void I had never known God's love. As a child I had never possessed God's truth. In the absence of such truth, the void was filled with lies. Abuse soon followed, and I had no means of dealing with such violence. Turning back to God's truth has been the only way to reclaim the living stream that flowed with freedom and potential.

I knew there wasn't any sadness in heaven. I was aware that Mum had felt remorse for her sins in order to repent of them. Some people say that if God forgives us, then why not live as we please and ask for forgiveness when the time comes? The truth is that none of us know when our time will come. When it does, I would rather have Jesus vouch for me, instead of trying to explain away a life of ignorance, selfishness, and repeated mistakes. That would be too terrifying a prospect to face.

There were times through the prayers and chats when I needed to scream at Mum about how wrong she had been. God allowed me to say everything I needed to say, releasing every crippled emotion. I imagined myself in Mum's place, responding to the world she knew. Who knows what damage had been done to her? I experienced all the pain that God knew I could stand. I didn't simply talk my way through this, and God didn't let me fumble my way through it. His gentle sorting of my chaotic mess made forgiving Mum possible.

God worked at a remarkable speed. I only prayed and chatted with Christine once a week for a month. In this time, I was taught to mourn for the child robbed of her innocence and to cry for the teenage rape victim. I cried to God, 'I've been robbed for so long by these boys that I refuse to be robbed any more. Father, don't let me cry any more, don't let this go on any longer than you want it to. As soon as you have finished this work in me and taken me through that room, clear out all the old muck and fill it again with you. Then I want to leave here.' I didn't want to hold on to the pity that God had released in me for thick and ugly Mandy Curtis, the gypsy and the slut.

God doesn't just remove the rubbish from our lives; he replaces it with gold. He takes our narrow, tainted perspective, and replaces it with his perfect wide-screen vision. He replaced the loveless pain of that filthy room with a husband-to-be who would love me. In hindsight, I could see how the day of Carol's daughter's christening had been a day from God, in that I had time to bond with Mum before she died. When my days revolved around drugs and abuse, Jenny Quaif had prayed for me. In the most desperate hour I have ever tasted, Callie had felt God prompt her to send me an invitation to church, a simple gesture. I saw a divine parallel between the evil of rape committed by two boys, and the restoration of love and trust in the arrival of two male Christian friends, Tim and Augie. God had been slowly undoing twisted knots and changing my tangled beliefs. I began to see just how valuable I was to Jesus. He had saved me from death by taking all my sins to his cross, and now he wanted the relationship with me that I was originally designed to prosper in.

At Elim, the pastor spoke about the heart and love of a father. It was a very powerful and emotional service. He ministered to those who had not had the father they needed, and especially to those whose fathers had rejected them. It can be difficult for people to accept the love of God as the heavenly Father, when their own father has caused them rejection and pain. I was touched by what God was leading him to say, because I was sad at having missed out on that vital relationship.

In response to the service, I thanked God for being my Father, and as I prayed, a great weight fell from my shoulders. I had agonised over the details of who my father was for years. As a teenager, I had often looked at men in the street, wondering if one of them was the man who left Mum's house-warming party. I'd lay on my bed dreaming of what he was like, and what we would talk about when we met. He had become my most secret dream; he would make my world better, my saviour astride a white horse. Now I could finally let go of that dream. It was a great relief to say to God that I no longer needed to know who my father was.

The following day, I cried silent and hollow tears. Although I had confirmed God's parental love over my life, I had unearthed a deep and dried-up well inside of me. From the beginning of our relationship, I had been open to God's fatherly love. No human being could match my childhood fantasy of what this Greek hero of a father would be like. God, in his magnificence, not only met my expectations, but also exceeded them. He had free reign to be my only father, because he had my full attention as a daughter.

A new couple had joined our church. Augie and I had been giving out invitations to church in the town centre, and the new couple came to Elim as a result. They had both moved from Spain to England to train as nurses. The man was English, and his father was the pastor of an evangelical church in Spain. His parents had travelled from Spain to visit him. One morning at Elim, his father was called to the front of the church to introduce himself. In tears he said, 'It wasn't until I saw my son that I realised how much I have missed him, and how much I have needed to see him. God knows our needs more than we know ourselves.'

As soon as I heard this, God said to me, 'And I know how much you need to meet your father.'

I remembered thinking I didn't need to know, and this time I cried real tears. God showed me the truth behind my thinking, making me transparent, exposing my desire.

'I don't need to know,' I'd said to God in prayer.

'Yes you do!' came the divine correction from the Voice of Truth.

That evening, I went home to Christine's and cried uncontrollably. I shared a room with Danielle and didn't want to wake her, and so I buried my face in the pillow. I called repeatedly, 'Daddy, Daddy,' and as I did, God took me back to the time when as a little girl I had begged Mum to tell me who my dad was, but she had refused. Over the years that unanswered question had suffocated a part of me. Buried inside of me was a father's daughter, a daddy's girl, who had never been allowed to live.

God opened the floodgates, and although my heart was aching from the pain, I could feel his protection over me. I repeated the childhood cry for my dad. I couldn't stop. God allowed me to cry what I had needed to on the day I was silenced by Mum. I had been stopped from growing, from feeling and from mourning. As I cried out, 'Daddy', God said, 'Don't be ashamed. You say this as many times as you need to.'

Whenever God released these emotional earthquakes, I was left shaken. The epicentre was painful and raw. The aftershocks came in the revelation that I hadn't known the pain existed. The abortions, the rape, Mum and now my father – I had beckoned God to do his work. I had asked him to break me, so that I could bless people and bring them to his kingdom. What good would I be in pointing people towards God, while dragging behind me sacks of abused emotions? I needed God's prescribed healing.

The world of spiritualism teaches us to meditate on our inner selves. It points towards self-improvement and fulfilment in the oneness of nature and the energy of the universe. Self-improvement is worthless if I am still living outside of God's will. Spiritual healing is sickness if I am still entrenched in sin and separated from God. I look to God's healing because I don't want my future to be robbed by my past. And right then, my future lay with Tim.

Around this time, Tim and I led a church discussion group. One particular evening we were talking about God as Father, and the difficulties some people find in relating to God in this way because of their own negative experiences with their fathers. That night, many people responded to the need to see God as Father.

After we'd prayed with them, a lady came up to me and said, 'You know, you've been blessed in not knowing your father.'

I said, 'What!' I was angry, thinking that she didn't understand my pain of not knowing. But as much as that was true, as I reflected on what she'd said and, watching other people's struggles, I could see how I had a free path to my heavenly Father purely because I had nothing else to compare him with . . . apart from my childhood dream that my dad would be my saviour!

14

Pushing Forwards

It was more than just a compliment. When Tim and I first started going out together, the first people he shared the news with were his parents.

'People spend their whole lives looking for that perfect woman,' Jen told her son, 'and you have already found her.'

I knew that I was far from perfect. But Jen's words were a different language to the words spoken over me as a child. I took her comment as a special blessing from a special woman. With this in mind, I waited for God's appointed date with expectations of a wonderful day.

I asked Christine Beales's husband John if he would give me away at the wedding. I could have asked either of my eldest sisters, Lynn or Carol, and I worried about them feeling pushed aside, but John was a kind man. I wanted a father, even if it was only for a day; for a father-figure to escort me on my wedding day encapsulated part of the fairy tale. This was God's day, an occasion where he wanted the best for me, and I wanted to walk towards my husband-to-be with a father by my side. It meant a lot to me that John was willing to see me as his daughter.

111

My family was equally supportive. Lynn had got to know Tim before the wedding, and she made the cake. All my sisters were present, as well as my auntie and my nan. We asked people to bring food and to simply be a part of the celebration. Around two hundred and fifty people turned up to share the day. People stepped forward to pray for us, including my nan, who was a churchgoer, and I knew this must have been odd for my sisters to witness. It is hard for people to understand prayer until they first understand the need to pray. Prayer is not wishful thinking, conjuring, or spell-casting in any shape or form. It is direct communication with the living God and, as a parent listens to the needs of their children, God listens to our needs. Whether the guests celebrated with or without this knowledge, it was still a celebration of God and his covenant of marriage. It was a wonderful day in which everyone I loved shared a brief moment of time together.

I had longed to be part of a family, and now I was a part of Tim's. Jen and Bernard would talk for hours with Tim and me. We talked about our relationship with God as well as our individual hopes and dreams. Jen would phone Tim if we hadn't seen them for a week, and being included in this way was the opposite to how I grew up, dismissed and ignored. I thanked God for Tim and his family, but these early days of marriage were insecure times for me. At first, Tim and I spent every evening together, but the honeymoon didn't last. When I felt that Tim was spending too much time on his work, I began to panic. I didn't know how a husband and wife should function together. My expectations were derived from romantic movies, in which film stars played out multi-million dollar Hollywood fantasies.

It was hard making the adjustment from being Amanda Curtis to becoming Amanda Lord, and my old fears of rejection came flooding back. I became paranoid, and kicked back at Tim for not spending every living moment with me. I screamed, shouted and threw things at him, physically and verbally. He wasn't giving me the kind of attention I'd seen in movies! My relationship with God was fantastic; I would pray and be used by the Holy Spirit to speak into someone's life. But in my sin, my broken human condition, my insecurities and anger found an outlet against my husband. Throughout this period of testing the marital waters, Tim was wonderful. God said he would be, and against all my fears of rejection, Tim continued to love and accept me.

We had spoken our wedding vows before God. We had invited him to be the third strand of the cord binding us together as husband and wife. This is the spiritual bond between a man and a woman as God intended. According to God, a woman is to submit to her husband as the church submits to Jesus. And a man is to love his wife, as Jesus loves his church. Tim loved me because he knew the love of Christ, and he strove to reflect it. He didn't reject me; he was calm and patient. However, the change that marriage had brought to my life stirred something inside me. I was unsettled, searching spiritually, but I didn't know what for.

Not long after the wedding, I spent a morning speaking at my nan's church. The congregation consisted of around twenty little old ladies, but their faith was vibrant. My nan put out the flowers and made the tea on a Sunday morning. I shared my testimony of how I had come to know God, and my Christian vision to see other people find their relationship with him. Afterwards, I spoke to Nan about God recognising our hearts behind the smallest acts of devotion – even in what some would consider insignificant, like making the tea. If it is done because of our love for God, then it enables him to bless others.

Then, Nan told me something amazing. She said that when Mum was dying and they had slept in the same room together, she had prayed with Mum and Mum had given her life to Jesus. I remember Mum being thrilled, because it was the first night she had slept properly in months. Nan had prayed with Mum to ask God to forgive her! I told her about the vision I had been given about Mum. Listening to Nan was a powerful confirmation that Mum had been saved.

I had once cried out to God when I had wanted to die, but Mum had been literally dying. Her body was winding down towards its last intake of oxygen and its last functioning heartbeat. What did she have to cling to any more when pride, success, failure, anger and hurt would all be cancelled in one defining moment of death? God had battled for her, never once withdrawing his love and grace. Nan had prayed with Mum to open her eyes. She knew that every moment of Mum's life had been of supreme value to God, and at the eleventh hour, Mum had called out to Jesus.

While Mum had suffered from cancer, Tim's mum, Jen, was fighting her own battle with the same illness. Tim and I asked God to heal her completely, believing that he would. Now I had found such a loving family, I would not let the thought of her dying enter my head. When Tim and I returned from our honeymoon, Jen was in a wheelchair because her bones were brittle. Bernard was angry about Jen's condition. It was an anger directed towards the doctors. As Jen visited the cancer hospice for treatment, her physical deterioration became obvious. She became paralysed from the waist down, and at times was so sick she could barely move, receiving physical rejuvenation through the necessary blood transfusions. Even in the last stages of her illness we believed for a miracle, claiming that God would heal her as he had healed others.

At the cancer hospice, Bernard did not leave his wife's side. He cared for her and loved her, taking on board most of the work that the visiting nurses were paid to do. He dressed and cleaned her bedsores as part of a daily routine; some of the sores had eaten through to the bones in her legs. We never knew what to expect each time Jen had to visit the hospice.

One morning, as Tim and I were staying at Bernard's house, the hospice requested our presence because Jen did not have much longer to live. Tim ran from the house to be with his mum and I followed soon after. I arrived only to watch her die. Jen looked unbelievably peaceful, with no fear in her expression. God's presence filled the hospice room, and I marvelled at the fact that Jen was now with him. I had felt God's touch and could not live without it; whatever fulfilment Jen was experiencing lay beyond my comprehension.

I felt deeply for Bernard and his family. It was exceptionally hard watching them survive their loss. If there was ever a tear I shed for myself, it was because any children I had would grow up without a grandmother. Jen was a spiritually strong mother, close to God and receptive to his influence. She would have made a gifted grandmother. It felt like such a waste that she would not fully fulfil this role. I was greatly encouraged by some words from the book of John:

> I tell you the truth, unless a grain of wheat falls to the ground and dies, it remains only a single seed. But if it dies, it produces many seeds. (Jn. 12:24)

Faced with having to sift through the rubble caused by death, I tried to work through it logically. I thought the best thing God could have done was to heal Jen. It would have provided a powerful miracle for the church that had prayed for her. It would have encouraged their faith for when such a tragedy struck at the heart of another family. When I had believed for Jen's healing, it had not been for my sake, but for her older son Simon and her daughter Andrea. I believed that when they saw God's miracle of healing, they would come running to him. I tried to work God out, as to how he should best conduct himself in our mortal world. I knew he could have healed Jen instantly; he could have raised her from the dead if he had wanted to, but it had not been his will.

I had to stand on the fact that there are no accidents with God. Nothing escapes his control. He allows disease, illness, violence, abuse, rape and death. These terrible things have God's permission to exist, because when we rejected his Father's embrace we chose the breakdown of his created order. God allows us to temporarily live side by side with evil. But in his perfect will he wants us to choose to love him and live with him beyond death, where the fatal effects of sin will no longer be able to harm us. Is it really too far-fetched to believe?

In the Western culture of deep-rooted cynicism, despite the distrust and mockery of the supernatural, people would rather believe in anything than Jesus the Son of God, sacrificing his life to save ours. The name Jesus means 'the Lord saves'; God sent his Son to save us, to rescue us from ourselves and to bring us into a friendship with him. I cannot work God out but I don't have to. He has already explained who he is and what he wants through the perfect example of Jesus.

Jen had made the decision to live with God instead of without him. When she died his presence was tangible.

Jen's physical departure, despite being an event to mourn, became a seed for God to sow.

With everything to live for, Tim and I decided to start a family of our own and I became pregnant within a week of stopping contraception. Tim was excited about the news that he would soon be a father and I knew that he would make a fantastic dad. He had a gentle demeanour and knew instinctively how to deal with children, inheriting that particular gift from his mother. Both Jen and Bernard had been great with Danielle, and Tim's relationship with her had always been strong. I was excited for Tim. I already knew how wonderful the miracle of pregnancy was; the sequence of events that God puts into motion, the growth from nothing, the baby kicking, the bond between mother and child. I couldn't wait to watch Tim go through the anticipation of approaching parenthood.

The baby was due on 15 October 1998, and because Danielle had been a week early, I convinced myself that this baby would be another early arrival. I had only gained a stone in weight with Danielle, but this time I almost tripled in size. I had discovered from my first scan that it was a boy, and we had already chosen the name Ethan Bernard: Ethan means 'solid and enduring' or 'pushing forwards consistently', Bernard means 'like a bear'. The pregnancy wasn't complicated, but it did have its problems. Ethan was lying on a nerve, which caused me a lot of pain, and he seemed determined not to come out. It felt like the longest pregnancy in the world. Pushing forwards was the last thing he did, and if he was like a bear, he was in hibernation. Ethan was sixteen days late and determined not to live up to his name.

I had a friend called Teresa who I had met at a children's playground. We started chatting as Danielle played with her daughter. Teresa was going through the emotional turmoil of a divorce. I talked freely to her about God's influence over my own turbulent past. She admitted to wanting the same peace that God had given to me. One day we were sitting in the car together and I prayed silently, 'Lord, if it's right that Teresa attends church on Sunday, I pray that she will ask me.'

I was fed up of being knocked back for my faith, and I didn't want to push her for a response. Teresa did ask, and she gave her life to Jesus in the very first church meeting she attended. It had been worth praying. Teresa and I developed a close and trusting friendship, and so I asked her to help me at Ethan's birth. Tim was completely supportive, but he didn't like hospitals. He might have been there to look after me, but I needed Teresa to look after him!

Ethan Bernard Lord was born an hour and a quarter after my waters broke. Tim, the father, held his son, and from that moment Ethan reclined in a pose of complete serenity. The midwife commented at how amazed she was at the peace in the room. We had all felt it. Ethan was laid-back and calm, only waking in the night to chuckle and make cooing sounds. I would wake before him and wait for him to open his eyes; he was an absolute joy. Tim said that as soon as he saw his son, he felt the spiritual light of fatherhood being switched on. How much more must God as the perfect Father look forward to another life, another child, and another generation rich in hope.

Danielle loved her brother straight away, and Bernard was ecstatic at the sight of his grandson. Ethan's birth reinforced how much we were all missing Jen, but it also brought a new joy and focus to the family. Despite the loss and grief that had been inflicted, a seed of hope and potential had been sown. I was getting to know Tim's brother, Simon, and as soon as Ethan was home from hospital, I was introduced to his girlfriend Gemma. They began to visit regularly. I could feel that God was at work behind the scenes of Bernard's family.

One weekend, Tim was away working and my friend Teresa came over to stay. We spent a while praying together, and in a moment of silence, we listened for God's voice in the quiet stirring of our hearts. We both felt that one day we would meet our fathers. I was amazed that God had planned this. When Tim returned, I told him everything in a shower of excitement. He said to keep it in my heart, because if it was God's will, then it would certainly happen.

Although I hadn't asked him to, God continued to feed my spirit by speaking about my father. Through the simple routine of housework, or the demands of the children, he would prompt me continuously. I could be praying for something completely different, and suddenly I would hear him say, 'I am going to restore your family. You will meet your father one day.' It was a promise. God said it would happen.

He whispered his vision, and I felt as if I was being pampered by his promise. I saw a clear picture of myself embracing a man, and God would tell me, 'This is your father.' Even while lost in my own fuzzy collection of thoughts, God would bring his vision to the forefront of my mind. I knew that God wanted me to share and believe in his dream, and as I dared to dream again, my level of faith and expectation increased.

As more people arrived at the church, I made new friends. Amanda Hills had been pregnant at the same time as me, and her son was born a few months before Ethan. We immediately connected and shared our testimonies over lunch. We both felt that we were destined to meet.

'You know what?' I announced, 'God has told me that one day I am going to meet my dad.'

Amanda listened and then added, 'I believe that too.'

I knew from that moment, that this was a divine friendship; we were able to confide, pray, laugh and cry in the safety of God's presence. We prayed for each other's lives and for my father. As a result, God built up our faith, which according to the Bible is the evidence of things unseen. Based on this evidence, I felt God say that it was now time for me to start pushing forwards to search for my father.

Part III

Shifting Sands

15

Twisted Road

I needed to find a handful of facts amid the minefield of rumours. I knew that Lynn's father, Stelios, had introduced my parents at a party, but this had become obscured behind layers of speculation. There had even been talk of Stelios being my uncle, which would make Lynn and I cousins as well as sisters. I needed to ground this search in truth. The truth was that apart from my mum, only two people knew my father's identity. Stelios had moved to Australia and had lost contact with his daughter Lynn, which left Lynn's uncle, Paul, who used to visit the house when I was a child.

I remembered how once, at sixteen, Mum took me out for a surprise. We caught the bus to Eastbourne to meet Carol, and Mum took us to a restaurant for a meal. I knew the owner was Greek, and I thought that Mum was going to reveal the secrets surrounding my shadowy heritage. I watched the owner interact with Mum; he was a little Greek man called Nicky who was married to an English lady. Over the meal, Mum told us that she had worked for him when Lynn was a baby. I wondered whether he knew who my father was. Nicky was a Greek Cypriot, and seeing his restaurant, I became aware of the Greek legacy in Eastbourne.

My first step from prayer to the practical was to visit my sister Lynn. When Tim and I arrived at Lynn's, without me saying a word, she told us that she wanted to contact her father in Australia. This was no coincidence, but I didn't say so to Lynn; she would have thought I was mad. After talking, Lynn and I agreed to search for our missing fathers together.

I made a further arrangement to visit Lynn. She knew a man called Anthony who owned another Greek restaurant in Eastbourne. On the strength of the prayers Amanda Hills and I had offered to God – to open doors and bring us a miracle – I visited the restaurant with Lynn to talk to Anthony the Greek.

'How is your Mum doing?' asked Anthony.

'Mum has passed away,' Lynn responded.

'Oh, I'm sorry to hear that.'

'That's OK, thanks for asking. Actually, we've come to pick your brains about something.'

I explained to him who I was, and asked him if he knew my father. All I knew was that my father's name was Terry, and that he knew Stelios. Unfortunately, Anthony could not shed any more light on our situation. But when I asked him whether he knew Stelios's brother, Paul, he said, 'Yes.'

He offered to ring Paul on our behalf and ask him for the information that we both needed. Anthony suggested that Paul might in fact be my father, but I snapped back with a defiant 'No!' Paul used to visit the house and give us money, but I believed that Mum would have told me if I had been his daughter. Lynn and I left the restaurant feeling triumphant. It had all been so easy. God had promised that I would meet my father, and so I anticipated the next episode with confidence.

I sat back and waited for Anthony to phone. After a couple of weeks' silence, I decided to ring him at his restaurant.

'Hello, Anthony,' I said, 'I hope you're not busy. But I was wondering if you'd managed to contact Paul?'

'Oh yes. I was about to get in touch with you,' came his reply. 'I've spoken with him. But you really don't want to contact your father. I found out that his name is Peter, he lives in Canada, and he's part of the Mafia out there. He actually has men guarding his home with machine-guns!'

I laughed.

'But my mum told me his name was Terry,' I responded. 'And even if he is part of the Mafia, that wouldn't stop me wanting to meet him!'

I didn't know whether Paul had fed Anthony this rubbish, or whether Anthony had made it up all by himself. The lie was ridiculous, but the reason behind it had upset me. If they didn't know who my father was, then why didn't they say so? Instead, they had either tried to divert or stop my search altogether. Why did they want to throw me off the scent so dramatically? Fortunately, Anthony the messenger was not my only lead, and so he was quickly dropped from my list of enquiries.

During prayer, Amanda Hills saw a picture of me trapped inside a chrysalis. It was an image inspired by God, and through it he explained that although it appeared like he was doing very little, one day I would break out and fly. I was inspired by a quote from the Bible. It was Psalm 139, written by King David who as a boy defeated the giant Goliath. I reflected on the psalm, that 'all the days ordained for me were written in [God's] book before one of them came to be' (v. 16). In God's eyes, I had never been a mistake, and neither had my father. There was a plan and a purpose to every facet

of my life. I was also pointed towards the Gospel of
Matthew:

> You are the light of the world. A city on a hill cannot be
> hidden. Neither do people light a lamp and put it under
> a bowl. Instead they put it on its stand, and it gives light
> to everyone in the house. (Mt. 5:14,15)

I had always been hidden; people had hidden me from
the truth, from my father, and from the world. I remembered, as a child, being in a car with Mum and my sister
Bev. We drove past a wedding, and as the guests took
their photographs of the happy couple, I saw Lynn's
uncle Paul. I was about to shout at him through the window, but Mum grabbed hold of my head and shoved me
down out of sight. I was hidden, but why? God revealed
these pieces of the puzzle, and then spoke into them
with his word of living power, his breath of life. The
world pays a fortune for therapy and counselling, and
some of it is not without merit, but nobody is qualified
to match God's understanding. Who better to speak into
our lives than God who created us? He alone has
planned our yesterday, today and tomorrow before we
were even born.

Lynn and I arranged to visit Nicky, who Mum had
once worked for. He was genuinely pleased to see us
and most upset about Mum's illness and death. Lynn
asked whether there was any way he could find her
father's phone number. Nicky was excited about helping. He told us that the owners of the neighbouring
restaurant were related to Stelios, and he offered to talk
to them about our search. I asked him about my own
father, feeling that this lead was far more positive than
the last. As it happened, Nicky remembered a Greek
man with a similar name who worked as a chef at the

hospital in Eastbourne. Our meeting concluded as Nicky said he would be in contact within the next couple of weeks; all we had to do was wait.

I waited for the phone call, but again nothing happened. These early steps were making demands of my faith and stamina that I had not expected. One after the other, people made promises only to forget them, and I swayed from peace and enthusiasm to anxiety and frustration. Thinking about what Nicky had told me, I rang the hospital switchboard and asked for Theo who worked in the kitchen. A man came to the phone. Once again, I explained my identity, my story and my purpose. Referring to a possible one-night stand, in a Greek accent he said, 'Oh well, it could be me, love; in those days that's what we all got up to.'

I asked Theo whether I could meet him at the hospital. He agreed, and so I drove to Eastbourne with the possibility of meeting the father I had never known. On the way, I was caught in a two-hour traffic jam and I arrived at the hospital frantic with anxiety. I met Theo in the canteen and we sat down for a coffee. He looked at me with curiosity and said, 'I can tell which family you are from, but you do not come from mine.'

It was obvious to me that we were not related. Theo was a short, Greek man, who looked nothing like me. However, he was lovely, polite and encouraging. What amazed me was how, if we had been related, he would have accepted it. I was also surprised at being asked the same question again.

'Are you sure you're not Paul's daughter?' he said.

'No, I'm not Paul's daughter,' I replied. 'My mum wouldn't have lied to me. And if she had wanted to lie, she could've told me any story to fob me off.'

'Well, I don't know another Theo. But you're a lovely girl and I wish you well in your search.'

'Can you understand how I feel?' I said, as my continued disappointment expressed itself in tears.

'This is a hard road you have chosen,' he said. 'But if you want to try and find him, don't you give up. I can see the family you're from.'

Much to my despair, I began to doubt Mum's integrity. Had God been pointing me towards Paul all along? Had Paul's house calls and handouts held a deeper meaning than being casual visits? He had been married; I remember him and Mum heatedly discussing his views on female submission. Had his true relationship with me remained a secret because of his wife? It was no coincidence that two Greek men who didn't know me had both connected me to him. But the last thing I wanted to discover was that my mum had lied. I had dreamt that my father didn't know I existed and would be ecstatic upon finding out. The reality was that I had already embarked on a complicated and twisted road, currently snaking its way towards Lynn's uncle Paul.

As these possibilities and disappointments accumulated, I told God that the search was becoming too difficult. I doubted whether I could go through with it. My friend Amanda Hills and I continued to pray, and Tim was ever supportive. But I needed something a lot more solid than chasing after strangers in hospital canteens. Instead of relying on the promises of others, I needed to make contact with Paul myself. Nicky continued to offer his help, only to remain silent. Waiting for these men to call, men who were possibly a couple of phone calls away from ending my search, became almost impossible to endure. Eventually, Nicky spoke to the elusive Paul, who again fired the Mafia story at me. I thought that for Paul to conceal what he knew, meant that he was either very close to my father, or he was my father. That frightened me; I didn't want to doubt Mum's word. And I remembered Paul tried to seduce my sister. I didn't want this man to be my father.

When I read Psalm 139, I found myself with a couple of questions. If God knew every single day of my life, if I had never been hidden from his presence, then why had such terrible things happened? Why hadn't God revealed himself earlier? I wanted to be honest with God, because God wanted me to love him through all my praise and despair, and through all my faith and doubts.

Amanda Hills told me to imagine that I was looking at a photo album, and to allow God to speak as I flicked through the pages. So I visualised an album, and in my mind's eye I saw little freeze-frame pictures of my life. In each slice of my past God whispered, 'I was there.' There were even pictures of my father the morning after Mum's house-warming party. He was walking down the stairs and leaving the house. Again, God whispered, 'I was there.' It was his sovereign affirmation that nothing escapes him. Frame by frame, page by page, I saw that through both the good and the bad, not once had God left my side.

In the aftermath of tragedy, the world cries accusingly, 'Where is God?' He is right with us, suffering alongside us, sharing our pain. Even through my nightmare and torment of rape and abuse, God had been there, grieving for his creation. But he still loves us. By divine appointment, Jesus suffered violation and humiliation on the cross, to redeem his Father's creation. There is also a divine purpose behind our suffering, but we won't find it by bitterly shaking our fists at heaven and shaking our heads at God.

My nan's faith in her generation invited God to begin his work in restoring mine. She became a blessing at

Mum's deathbed, and in turn, knowing that Mum had been saved became a part of my own healing. If I chose to disobey God, how could I expect to be a blessing to Danielle? My greatest failure as a parent would be to shield my own daughter from the knowledge of God. That decision would not only damage Danielle, but also her children, and her children's children. As a Christian mother, instead of protecting Danielle from the world, I could prepare her for it by encouraging her own relationship with God. He would protect her. Without him, she and another generation of my family would stumble fearfully through life, struggling to hear God's voice in times of hardship and pain. Yet ironically, during the frustration of searching for my father, one of the things that kept me focused on God was Danielle.

Like my faith, God's call to search for my father was not a journey of convenience. All my family, including Mum, had been damaged by the rejection of not knowing their fathers. Through his grace, God was restoring a fatherless generation. Through my faith and obedience, I had been given an opportunity to help break that curse.

16

My Goliath

I was a desperate and dangerous girl, a potential threat to a community where secret mistresses and the lies that covered them were rife. I waited for another couple of weeks, but there was no phone call and no photograph. It felt like my stomach and heart had been torn out. But despite my hopelessness, God reassured me, 'It is going to happen, keep going, keep believing.'

I eventually received a phone call from Nicky. He gave me Paul's phone number. We discovered he owned a restaurant in London; it was a huge breakthrough after months of silence. Knowing that Paul was armed with the most preposterous lies, I was afraid to ring him at first. When I did phone him the conversation was brief. Paul said that he would find my father's number and return my call. As usual, nothing happened. Tim suggested that he should pay him a visit. Face to face and man-to-man, Paul might act differently. We rang his restaurant, asked for the address, and then Tim drove up to London to surprise him.

Tim found Paul sitting behind the counter of his restaurant. He introduced himself and explained that he was visiting on my behalf, helping me to look for my father. Paul's reaction was positive; he lavished Tim with a free meal and listened to the story of my search. He claimed that he would be delighted to help, admitting that he kept my father's address at home. Meanwhile, I had been praying with Amanda Hills that this meeting would prove productive, and that Paul would give us some information. Tim's meeting concluded when Paul promised to send me a photograph of my father. When Tim returned from London with this news, I could not hold back my excitement; it was fantastic. It would have been a very different story had I walked into Paul's restaurant.

Sometimes, as tempting as it was to take matters into my own hands, God would tell me to wait. I listened for his instructions, rising with excitement only to fall with frustration. Amanda Hills and I continued to ask God for his guidance. We knew he was with us because, as Jesus tells us, when two or more meet in his name, then he is present. Amanda told me that Paul was like Goliath, a fierce opponent that I would have to fight.

So Tim rang Goliath to remind him of the photograph he had promised. Paul denied that he knew my father, claiming that there were no photographs. I felt sick with anger. It hurt so much that this man could knowingly stand between a father and daughter. Paul had no intention of helping, and I had to confront this Goliath figure. But as Paul's lies twisted and turned to suit the contours of the battlefield, I became too exhausted to fight.

Spiritually, I had entered the arena of Satan, the Prince of Lies, but God was fighting on my behalf. The confrontation began with a phone call. I explained to Paul that his dismissal was unacceptable; I was not stupid and I was not about to give up. All I wanted from him was the information to move beyond stalemate. It took all of my energy to speak to him. Paul replied with a cool confidence, 'OK, I'll send you what you want to know.'

Goliath stood his ground. Nothing arrived.

I felt like I was drowning in Paul's mire. It took all my strength to claw at the surface to gasp for air. My spiritual resources were drained, and even church began to take a turn for the worse. The meetings began to lack freedom as the church focused on its recovery. I missed the limitless breath of the Holy Spirit and I stopped dancing.

On Ethan's first birthday, I announced to the family that I was pregnant again. I had desperately wanted another child. Danielle was now eight years old, and I was aware of the difference in age between my two children. I wanted Ethan to have a little brother or sister closer to his own age.

The Old Testament used to seem dated and irrelevant to me. Now it came alive. At that time, God inspired me to read the story of Joseph. He was betrayed by his own brothers and cast into an empty well while they decided on whether or not to kill him. He endured betrayal, humiliation and imprisonment, but it was all part of God's bigger plan. As I read the story, I knew that God was drawing me out from my own deep well of emotional upheaval. I learned from Joseph that when God makes a promise, it doesn't mean it will be easy, but it does mean it will happen. Joseph suffered the pain of separation from his family, but ultimately it became God's glorious reunion, bringing life not only to Joseph's family but also to a nation. God always has a bigger picture in mind.

In the midst of all these struggles, Tim and I developed a relationship with his brother Simon, and his girlfriend, Gemma. They knew of our faith and observed as Tim and I struggled with church, while I was looking out for my father on the horizon. But they also witnessed our faith as we lived for God despite our changing circumstances.

The family grew stronger. Ethan provided plenty of love and focus for everybody, and eventually his little brother, Joseph, was born. Whereas I had feared another overdue baby, Joseph arrived on time. When Ethan was born, he had relaxed, to everyone's delight. Joseph (meaning 'may he add') growled with defiance first at me and then at the world. Joseph Timothy was hard work from day one, crying solidly for the first three months of his fiery infancy. He was demanding, but I knew he would make an exceptional little brother for Ethan.

As I sat at home one Sunday morning, a friend from Elim came to see me.

'We had a guest speaker at this morning's service,' she said. 'He started speaking directly into people's lives – as if he knew them.'

'That's exactly what I need right now,' I said.

I was desperate for God to replenish my fading hope. So I went to the evening service with Gemma in tow. In the middle of the service, the preacher confirmed the words that God had given me when I first became a Christian: 'He will mightily bless you, and you will bring many people to his kingdom.' The preacher continued, saying that I would also teach people about God. I would stand on a platform speaking to many people, and I was not to be ashamed of being an emotional person. My character and temperament were God's gifts to be used.

It was Gemma's first time at church, and she sat next to me listening intently. I knew I had not been the best advertisement for Christianity. It had been the most barren season of my Christian walk, a blistering wilderness. I was exhausted trying to sustain my belief in God's promise that I would meet my father. I felt far away from God. Tim and I were struggling as a young family, straining to meet financial demands. I became desperate rather than inspired. On the way home, Gemma expressed her astonishment at what the preacher had said. She had heard him speak so personally about my character when he had known nothing about me. My vision had become choked by all that was happening but Gemma could see in me the woman of faith the preacher had described. In turn, I recognised in Gemma the spark of expectation that God gives people when he draws near.

We attended a prayer meeting together and Gemma discovered a genuine spiritual hunger. She was open to God and wanted to know him.

Tim's brother, Simon, was fighting his own battle with God. When Jen died of cancer, Simon had witnessed the Christian activity surrounding her death. He had felt indignant about their prayers for healing, especially as his mother had died. But it was the family's continued praise for God despite her death that shocked him. For years he had been looking for something this real. Not long after Gemma, Simon committed his life to Jesus Christ. There was a powerful seed growing from Jen's death. It was wonderful to be a part of God's movement and change.

As I ran my exhausting race, Amanda Hills stood on the sideline encouraging me not to give up. God inspired me to start recording my search in a diary. I also wrote a letter to Paul explaining how important it was for me to meet my father. I even said that I was beginning to believe Paul was the man I was looking for. I posted it and waited for a reply. Meanwhile God held his hand of peace and authority over my frail emotions.

I began to chronicle my journey, thanking God for carrying me and for not letting me go. The Bible states that anyone who trusts in God will not be put to shame. I asked for more faith to trust in his promise; I sensed that God would give me more opportunity to speak out against the lies of those who defied him. I asked God to help me overcome my weakness, by showing me my life from his perspective. He inspired me to write that 'if a seedling tree has to fight its way up through stones and hard soil to reach the sunlight, if it then wrestles with storms and frostbite to survive, I can be sure that its roots will be strong and its timber will be valuable'.

I struggled with the pain of my pleas being ignored by Paul, and I asked God to restore my vision of Jesus. God told me to clothe myself with Jesus, and that through faith and patience I would inherit the Promised Land. God directed me to run his race with patient endurance and active persistence. He would run ahead of me and never leave me.

The practice of writing my diary and Paul's letter, talking to God and reading his Bible, were all part of the fight against the enemy's lies. Amanda Hills rang and said that she felt that I should write Paul another letter. I was shocked, and protested, 'No, I don't feel I can do that. It would feel like I was begging. If Paul is my dad, then I don't want to know because he's a liar and a coward.'

God guided me in what to do. He spoke to me through the story of the persistent widow in the Gospel of Luke. The widow who had been wronged demanded justice from the judge. The judge did not care about her case, but her persistence drove him mad until he settled the matter for her. If the godless judge could be just, then how much more would God the Father who loves his people, provide his justice? (See Lk. 18:1–8.) I needed to push Paul to the point of frustration. I wrote another letter containing the direct accusation that he was my father, because otherwise why would he persist in lying?

One night, the children were in bed and Tim had gone out. I turned off the television and cried to God, 'It's been nearly three years now. Please tell me who my father is!'

I was alone at the foot of his throne, looking for his justice, seeking his answer, because he was my judge. I felt as though I had been spinning around blindfold and now I wanted to see again. I called out to God in tongues, words wrenched so deep from the depths of my spirit, that only God's Spirit within me could express them. I imagined that my cry of pain would never end. Then God removed the blindfold, and told me in a clear voice that in the next couple of days I would know my father's name. I danced with joy around the room.

The following day Amanda Hills and I met to pray together. She placed her hands over my ears, and I heard God say, 'Tomorrow you will know your father's name.' His presence was so strong that I fell flat on my back as waves of his peace washed over me. I shook with joy and held my arms out to him. He spoke again: 'What I am about to do in your life, you will declare to many nations.'

Names of countries flashed through my mind; one of them was Cyprus. I saw that God's plans were bigger than anything I was capable of understanding. That was why it had been so hard. Amanda Hills prayed that God would stretch my faith, pull my spiritual muscles, and lead me way beyond my search for a father.

I woke up the next morning and wrote in my diary: 'Today is the day I will know my father's name.' By writing it, I was declaring it in front of Jesus and his angels; this was the truth because God had spoken it. I also declared it to Tim, who had been with me through all my tears and joy. He looked at me and said, 'I hope so, for your sake.'

I waited all afternoon, but nothing. Then at six in the evening, as Tim walked in from work, the phone rang. It was Paul, agitated and annoyed at the accusations in my second letter.

In a stumbling torrent of words, shaken from his detached confidence, Paul told me that I had no right accusing him of being my father. I fought back, telling him that because of his lies I no longer trusted anything he had to say. Paul, who had stood his ground for three long years, made his last stand as the mighty Goliath.

'There are four reasons why I am not your father,' he began. 'One, I never had that kind of relationship with your mother. Two, I was seeing someone else. Three, I wasn't even in the area at the time. And four, I know who your father is, and his name is Theodoros Antonios Selios.'

17

Wilderness Days

It was my time to dance, for now I had my father's name.

I rang Nicky, who had become my most reliable Greek contact and friend. Upon hearing my father's name he immediately recognised the connection. Theo, or 'Terry', had once worked in Nicky's restaurant. In fact, Nicky, Theo and the brothers Paul and Stelios had all grown up together in the same village in Cyprus. Nicky had Theo's address, and to pre-empt any more waiting, I said that I would meet him in Eastbourne to talk to him.

It had been about four years since God had told my friend Teresa and me that we would both meet our fathers. Despite Teresa's battle with the fact that her father had known about her, God brought them together. It was a privilege to be present when they met, and the reunion encouraged my own search. I read through the lists of names in the Bible, records that focused on the ancestry of Israel and Jesus. I had always found these parts of the Bible tedious to read, but God said that knowing where we come from is important to him. I was not to be ashamed that he had made wanting to know my father important to me.

I drove to Eastbourne to see Nicky. When he saw me again, he recognised the similarities between Theo and me, especially my eyes and smile. We shared a meal together and Nicky, inspired by my persistence, proclaimed his support.

'Look at your face,' he said, 'you can't stop smiling, can you? I should have realised who your dad was when I first saw you. Your eyes are the same as his.'

'It's amazing to finally have his name!' I responded.

That night as I left for Worthing, I had my father's address in my hand and a plan to write him a letter. With some help, I composed the letter explaining who I was. I based the letter on the facts rather than my feelings, because I was concerned about how he and his wife would feel. Instead of sending him an emotional tidal wave from a daughter he never knew existed, I stated clearly that I only wanted a chance to meet him. Included in the letter were photographs of me, Tim and the children.

Nicky told me that Theo lived in the Cypriot village of Ayios Theodoros, near Larnaca. It has one post office and one café. The villagers collect their own post, which sits in a sack at the back of the office. He warned me that it could take weeks for my father to receive the letter, and weeks for him to reply, depending on when he collected his mail.

I imagined this tiny fairytale island, populated by beautiful, dark-haired people, and fringed with white sand – but where the post may never actually arrive. As I sent the letter, I prayed that it would reach his hands.

Nicky's warnings were not without foundation, as I heard nothing for the next month. During these periods of expectation God provided me with his peace. When I lost that peace, becoming impatient and agitated, I took this as a nudge to take the next step. Having prayed for further guidance, I rang Nicky, who was going on holiday to Cyprus. He suggested that I wrote another letter; this time he would personally deliver it to my father's hands. I gave Nicky a second letter, taking him at his word, and prayed that he would encourage my father to act on it.

Again I waited, until one day Nicky rang the house. I greeted him, and he told me his story. He had visited the café in the village where he and my father had played together as children. He asked the owner to ring Theo and tell him that Nicky wanted to see him. The owner, acting as the messenger, conveyed Theo's response. Nicky was informed that Theo knew what the visit was about and he was not interested.

I had waited for years on a promise I believed was from God, and I believed I was closer than ever to communicating with my father. It was not to be. This became the lowest part of my journey, and I felt completely devastated hearing that Theo simply wasn't interested. This meant that he had received my first letter; he had looked at the photographs of his daughter and grandchildren, and he had chosen to remain silent.

I began to question my relationship with God. Had it been his voice and plan or had I been chasing my own imagination? God's promised reunion now felt overdue. Not only had I dragged my friends through all this drama only to let them down, I was also aware of being accused of wrapping all my faith up in my father and not in God. However, searching for my father had been God's vision, not mine. It had become mine only by trusting in God. He had planted and encouraged my need to know my father.

I had dreamt since childhood that when my father discovered he had a daughter, he would open his arms wide and be overcome with emotion. As a child, it was the dream that I held onto. Throughout the search, as each twist and turn darkened the childhood dream, I felt like the same child whose precious hope had been removed. It was God who wanted me to keep going and who knew the worth of what I was doing. But at times all I could feel was the intense pain and confusion.

I could place many things above God: my husband and children, my dreams, and make my life more comfortable and successful. But God says we should seek him first, with all our heart and strength, and that was what I was doing. At times, it meant hanging on to him by my fingernails. Once again I was inspired by the story of Joseph, and how God kept building Joseph up even in destitution. I told God that if he could teach me to believe in his promise, even in the depths of this pit, then I would never doubt him again.

After my own little Joseph was born, Tim and I moved from our council flat to a rented house with a garden.

One Sunday morning I left for church and immediately upon walking into the building, I felt convicted that I needed to be elsewhere. I longed to hear God's voice and feel the sweeping excitement of his presence in worship. There was a church in Littlehampton that had hosted the Cutting Edge events which had first inspired me to dance. I left for Littlehampton, arriving in time to hear a lady declaring the scripture that talks about how in the last days God will turn the hearts of the fathers towards their children. This was exactly what I needed to hear. God spoke to me in my spiritual wilderness, in the dry well I had been thrown in following my father's rejection of my letters. All I needed to know was that God had inspired the path I had been walking and he had not lost sight of his promise.

In fact, I was so inspired by feeling the presence of God again, that I returned to the same church a couple of weeks later. I had no longer felt part of the Christian community, part of the Spirit-filled body of Christ. As I stood in this new place of worship I felt in my heart that this was my home. When I shared this news with Tim, he was surprised and excited. He prayed about this change, asking God if we should move. The following morning Tim knew that following God meant moving to Arun Community Church as a family.

During our first visits to Arun we were welcomed and prayed for. We were also told that it would be a year of blessing for us. A few weeks later, a preacher stood at the front of the church with a pile of stones. He was talking about how everybody has a Goliath in their life, a situation that appears bigger than they can face. I was familiar with Goliath, and so I took a stone as a symbolic act, to tell God that I was still willing to fight for him. The preacher pressed the stone into my hand and I heard God say, 'Now I want you to go to Cyprus.'

Where God had once shown me a dark room, I now saw a second room, which was padlocked. It contained all the fear and pain that I had held on to concerning my father. Over the years, I had nurtured a bitter but comfortable emptiness. It was God's will to deliver me from this place of familiarity.

I imagined my father and me to be standing on opposite sides of a gaping chasm. Beneath us, a demonic army snarled and wailed, celebrating their triumph over my family, striving to keep us apart. I didn't want to give them any more ammunition than they already had. I needed to step away from the familiarity of rejection, learn how to be a daughter, and allow God to build his bridge towards my father.

I began to pray over God's instructions to go to Cyprus. Tim decided to stay and look after the children, especially with Joseph being so young and demanding. I needed a travelling companion and so I phoned my friend Christine Beales. She had previously travelled to China on mission work, and that very morning she had asked God for a new direction, and so she agreed to come to Cyprus. I could not think of anyone more suitable, because Christine had always stood by me when it came to believing God's promises. We booked our flight, and it transpired that I would be standing on Cypriot soil for my thirtieth birthday.

Tim and I committed ourselves to Arun Community Church, and we told our friends and our Elim pastor. By the time all the decision-making was over I was exhausted. I remember looking around at Arun. The church met in a school sports hall and the congregation numbered around four hundred and fifty people. At the heart of Arun are God and family. When the Father is invited to attend to his people, the children are not excluded, for they are part of the body of Christ. It is common to remove children from the main church service to a meeting of their own, enabling the adults to seek God in peace. However, I had already seen Danielle become bored and despondent with church. I prayed that she would find her relationship with God at Arun.

During the Sunday service before my trip to Cyprus, Ian McCormack, who I had previously watched on video, spoke from the stage. He was visiting the church, and he spoke with all the emotion and urgency of a man who had seen both heaven and hell. My mind was focused on Cyprus and my son Joseph, who I was trying to settle at the back of the congregation. Ian called out to me from the front. 'That girl over there in black. God has wanted me to speak to you for a while now. Come forward.'

I handed Joseph to Tim and walked to the front of the stage. Ian told me that I would become a blessing to marriages. This immediately brought God's peace to a turbulent river that had raged inside of me. Some sceptics had written off my search for a father as being indulgent and selfish. They failed to see God's perspective, accusing me of potentially wrecking my father's marriage and ruining his family reputation. I understood their doubts, but they only echoed the same sentiments that I'd heard from Mum. I became a secret because of Mum's pride in not wanting to wreck my father's marriage. I knew that when Ian said I would be a blessing to marriages, one of them would be my father's.

Nothing was going to stop me from crossing God's bridge to meet my father.

18

History Maker

As I looked at the clouds outside the window, tears ran down my cheeks. It was an emotional flight to Cyprus and I was grateful to have Christine by my side. While sitting on the plane God imprinted an image on my mind: I was holding out my hands, and he was filling them with little gifts. It had been the living God who had told me to start looking for my father. He had told me to fight Goliath, and he had told me when I would know my father's name. It was God who had taught me to believe for Cyprus – given me the faith to pray for the nation. Each of these gifts was like a small jigsaw piece, and each one was extremely valuable. The picture God was creating could not be completed without them. I knew there was more to come.

A friend of mine had given me a Walkman and some songs she had compiled on a tape. One of the songs was called 'History Maker' by the band Delirious?. I knew the song because I had followed the band since their early days at the Cutting Edge events on Littlehampton seafront.

On our first morning in Cyprus I sat on the hotel balcony while Christine slept. I listened as Delirious? sang about being history makers and speakers of truth. The words brought tears to my eyes as I reflected on what had brought me to another country in search of a stranger. God had placed his vision in me; it had begun as a daughter meeting her father. But it wasn't about me; it was about God and my father, God and my father's family, God and Cyprus. I got so carried away singing along to the track on the Walkman, that I woke Christine up!

We arrived in Larnaca armed with my father's name. Although we knew he now lived in Larnaca, we wanted to visit the village of Ayios Theodoros. Along with Paul and Stelios, this was the village my father had grown up in. Christine and I prayed, telling God that our time here was a blank canvas for him to paint. It was not for us to contrive anything that might conflict with God's picture for our visit. I already feared that in my own attempt to find Theo I could damage a delicate affair. This entire visit had to be God's timing, because only he could see the finished picture; I could only imagine it. Some might say it was foolhardy to be there in the first place with no idea of what to do next. But we saw it as an act of faith, because we had no idea what God was going to do next! We were the clueless English tourists and God was our divine guide.

The following morning, we walked around Larnaca to find somewhere that hired cars. As we wandered around in the Greek sun, we passed a taxi office. I asked the man in the office how much it would cost to drive to Ayios Theodoros. The man looked at me blankly and asked who it was that I knew in the village, because he himself lived there. I looked at Christine uncomfortably, and then back at the man, who could see that it was not a good question to have asked. Before I could stumble upon a coherent answer, he told me how much it would cost, saying that he would be glad to take us. He also added that anything I chose to tell him would be held in strict confidence. My mind was racing with questions of my own. Who was this man? Who might he know? Did he know my father, and should I tell him anything at all? We agreed that if he collected us at midday from our hotel and drove us to Ayios Theodoros, then I would tell him everything he wanted to know.

I walked away from the conversation in disbelief. My heart quickened as I wondered whether I was now potentially only a few hours away from meeting my father. Compared to the fight back in England, this venture into Cyprus had been refreshingly easy. I shared my excitement with Christine; we appeared to be in the final stages of my search. The taxi driver, whose name was John, arrived at midday to drive us to our destination. On the way, I told him why we had travelled to Cyprus. He answered excitedly that his wife knew Theo. She had been brought up in the same village, while John, despite being of Cypriot origin, had moved to Cyprus in his twenties. He looked at me with tears in his eyes, identifying with the pain of having Cyprus in the blood, only to remain a stranger. It was equally poignant for me to see my father's country and roots. I was spiritually connected to this land by Theo's blood, and yet all I had known was Mum's world of alienation and fear.

We were driven to Ayios Theodoros. John wanted us to meet his wife and mother-in-law, because they knew more than he did about my father's family. He drove us through the village, over dusty ground and past weathered houses. There was one café as Nicky had previously described, and an ancient church surrounded by trees rich with oranges. At the top of the village we stopped at a huge olive grove where John's family worked. He called out and I saw two beautiful Greek women with skin painted brown by the sun. The older lady was dressed in black and had a crown of shining white hair.

Both women were slightly embarrassed about being so sweaty from their work. They invited us to sit in a small hut, where we were served fresh lemonade and began to talk. They knew my father and told me how much I resembled him. I couldn't believe that I was at this stage of my journey; it was the highest peak of my search.

While our driver returned to Larnaca to work the rest of his shift, Christine and I agreed to wait in the village, as he offered to collect us later. We sat in the village and I cried, not through sadness, but because waves of yearning and emotion were breaking on these Cypriot shores. Christine was ever patient. She let me cry when I needed to, when I talked she listened, and when I needed advice she told me what she thought. She really had become a spiritual mother, providing me with care and support. Together we sat on a bench and watched the local children playing. The village had remained practically untouched by tourism; it was easy to imagine my father playing here as a child, as I had once played on the green. So little must have changed in the ancient village; even the shepherds still ushered their sheep through the streets.

I had brought with me the stone from Arun Community Church. It was my statement of how I was willing to fight for God's vision. There was a large pool of water in the village, in fact it looked like a lake, and I threw the stone into the water asking God to bring my father to me.

Christine said, 'Do you see the ripples? The fact that you are here today praying in this village is going to have a rippling effect, and it's going to keep moving.'

As I watched the ripples spread across the surface of the water, I reflected on the three long years of searching, and how my journey was almost over.

John the taxi driver returned and took us to his home, which on first appearance looked bleached to the point of being derelict. However, the inside was immaculate. It was so pristine that I could see my face reflected in the polished wood floor. We talked passionately about family connections. John's wife showed us photographs of my sister Lynn's father, Stelios, and a Cypriot sister Lynn didn't know existed. I told John's family about the people and events that had led me to Cyprus. Incredibly, John's wife knew Nicky from her own holidays in Eastbourne. I discovered that the two women were related to Lynn, and I wished my sister had been there to meet them herself. We had once agreed to look for our fathers together, but here I was without her. I became increasingly emotional looking through the photographs, and sat in silence while Christine talked to John's family. They were eager to help, and offered to find out where my father worked.

John drove us back to Larnaca. On the way through the village, he issued a warning: 'In a minute we are going to pass the only café in the village, and there's a man sitting outside. Pretend that you are just looking at the café as tourists, because that man is your uncle.'

I was so shocked that I looked straight at the man, and he looked straight back at me. We parked outside the café as part of John's sightseeing charade, and I held my uncle's gaze for about a minute before we continued home. John further revealed that my father worked in one of the hotels on Larnaca seafront. He left us, promising to contact us when he knew more. I had a feeling that we would be talking again very soon.

My thirtieth birthday fell on day two of our Greek adventure. I wrote in my diary: 'I believe this is the day that I am going to meet my father.' I prayed again with Christine, thanking God for this amazing pilgrimage to my Cypriot roots. Together we repeated our prayer for God's influence to ripple and pulse across the land. We were not going to storm into my father's life with accusations and demands – we recommitted ourselves to this. As followers of Jesus we wanted to move at God's pace, allowing him the sole authorship of this script.

I felt guilty that I had not been able to ask Lynn to accompany me on this trip, but prayer was integral to hearing God's voice. I needed somebody like Christine who could pray with the heart of a warrior, declaring God's authority over every situation. We were battling against the deception that had corrupted my family for a long time. I longed for Lynn to meet her family and discover this half of her ancestry and culture, but Lynn had said that I was mad for going in the first place.

We began our second day in prayer before venturing out for a walk. We reflected on a scripture from the story of Balaam in the book of Numbers:

> I could not do anything of my own accord, good or bad, to go beyond the command of the LORD – and I must say only what the LORD says. (Num. 24:13)

With this in mind, we quietly explored Larnaca only to become completely lost, wandering around the Greek resort. As we began to panic, John drove past in his taxi. He rescued us and took us back to his office, laughing that it was funny we should meet again as he was about to look for us at the hotel.

Larnaca seafront is a wall of whitewashed hotels, attracting holidaymakers to its exotic shores. The fruits of John's detective work revealed that Theo had worked in the very hotel Christine and I were staying in. John was totally overwhelmed at what he described as one coincidence after another unfolding before his eyes. My father had worked as a night porter, but left when his mother died only a few months ago. Our friend John believed it was fate that I would meet my father; I explained that it was in fact prayer. He became even more emotional when he found out it was my birthday, revealing to me that he had acquired Theo's phone number.

'Do you want to ring it?' he asked.

'Yes.' My heart pounded as I watched him wait for my father to answer. I looked at Christine and knew she was praying silently, and so I murmered under my breath: 'Please, pick up the phone.'

My father's wife answered. John introduced himself informally because they already knew each other. He asked if Theo was there; he was out, but he would be returning later that afternoon. He asked her if she would ask Theo to ring him on his return, and she agreed. When John put the phone down, we gave him a big hug. He may have attributed all this to fate, but he had remained faithful to his word by finding out about my father for me. His enthusiasm and help had gone beyond all our expectations.

Christine and I decided to occupy ourselves in Larnaca, and John said he would ring us after he had spoken to Theo. On my twenty-first birthday, God had saved my life. Nine years to the day, I was on the brink of meeting my father. This gift from God could only exist because of that first life-changing encounter. I owed it all to God. It would be his amazing victory.

As Christine and I explored Larnaca in the sun, we knew how dismal the weather would be in England that early March day. I felt peaceful and confident that the situation was in God's hands. I prayed that he would give John the right words to say to Theo. At half past six, John phoned our hotel and said that he had spoken to my father. Although Theo had not admitted to being related, he agreed to meet me because I had journeyed such a long way to see him. This was great news. Theo may have not acknowledged our relationship, but he had acknowledged my persistence in wanting to find him. He knew of my previous attempts because of the letter he had read and Nicky's visit. I hoped that all these elements would be enough to replace his fear with courage.

Christine ordered some food, and we ate my birthday meal at the hotel, waiting for the phone to ring. I was aware of the complications surrounding such a phone call. My existence had been shrouded in secrecy and lies. There was a possibility that my father would not ring immediately because of his wife – to admit to our relationship would mean admitting to an affair.

I spent the evening dreaming of what it would be like to finally meet him. I imagined him walking into the hotel and greeting me. I chronicled the events of my Cyprus visit, writing them down to remind me of what God had done.

I had arrived in Cyprus with my father's name and a passion to seek God's heart. God had placed us in the very hotel where my father used to work. I'd seen where he had played as a child and I had spent some time with my sister Lynn's family. I had seen my uncle, and had met John who had been an invaluable link in the chain, understanding my alienation in this land. He found my father's number and through speaking on my behalf, Theo had agreed to ring me. We had given God a blank canvas to work on, to be as receptive to his plan as we possibly could. This was how God chose to fill in his canvas. Everything had happened according to his design; I was about to meet my father.

19

Lazarus Heart

After the death of so many hopes and dreams, I was ready for a resurrection. On day three of our visit, after a few phone calls home to share my stories with Tim and Amanda Hills, we prayed again for God to lead us.

Christine had been reading about Lazarus, Jesus' friend whom he raised from the dead. Lazarus had inspired Christine, because upon walking from his tomb on Jesus' command, he then had to shed the clothes that had wrapped him in his grave. We prayed about the meaning of this; God can and will bring life to the dead, physically and spiritually. We prayed that he would breathe life into my relationship with my father.

While we were out walking, Christine and I came across a beautiful old church. We had to wear a shawl to enter because it was disrespectful to show any bare shoulder, and so we respected the local custom. Once inside we were shocked to see a plaque above an archway that read 'The Tomb of Lazarus'. We both felt God's Spirit inspire us as we stood by the tomb of the man Jesus resurrected. According to the history of this church, Lazarus sought refuge in Cyprus from persecution. When he died his second death, he was buried in a tomb in a small church. The decorative Byzantine church that we were standing in had not been constructed until the ninth century.

Lazarus, alive at the passionate command of the Son of God, had once inspired this small Cypriot body of Christ. What a church it would have been, far from the twenty-first-century tourist spot of today.

God is going to dig up the old, dry wells and make them flow again with water. After everything God had told us, finding this church was no coincidence. Together we marched around the building, asking God to raise it from the dead and restore it to its former vitality. We had tears in our eyes as we realised the magnitude of God's plan. His stone had been plunged into the depths of the lake, and the church, the village, and the nation were all caught in its succession of ripples.

There was still no phone call from the elusive Theo and our visit was drawing towards its end, but I felt it had no conclusion. All I wanted was a glimpse of my father's face. It was amazing to know his name from the tangle of phone calls and lies, and now to stroll down the sun-baked streets in which he lived and breathed. He was so close. He knew the hotel I was staying in, and I wondered whether he was watching me, to catch a glimpse of my face. I'd dreamed as a little girl of wanting to look my best, so that he would be proud of me. I longed to meet him.

While I waited for my father to phone the hotel, I made my own tearful and confused call to my husband.

'Nothing has happened, Tim – I don't know what's going on,' I cried down the phone.

'Why don't you just enjoy the rest of your stay and then come home?' he responded, wanting to protect me from further pain.

'But I suppose I should look at the positive things that have happened,' I tried to convince myself. 'We've made lots of good contacts. It hasn't been a total waste of time.'

I declared to Tim everything that God had inspired, from throwing the stone to marching around the tomb. As I proclaimed God's vision, it reinforced once again that this journey was not about my feelings. In my emotional weakness, I was ready to fly back home and forget it. I wanted to disengage myself from the pipe dream of having a father and leave this painful road behind. However, this journey was God's will, and when I gave my life to Christ, I said I would be obedient to his will. Waiting for phone calls in Cyprus was as tedious as waiting for phone calls in England. The climate may have been better, but the anxiety was the same.

When day six arrived, it was clear that my father had chosen to remain hidden. I was too upset to speak to our helpful friend John. Christine explained that we had heard nothing, and John was upset that our alliance had concluded without the ending we had all hoped for. The hours were running out. The time to return to England was drawing near. I had shared this journey with so many people, and I knew they were waiting to witness the outcome. I believed that God would keep his promise and deliver my father. But I feared returning home with my sister's words echoing in my mind: 'You're mad! Why are you going to Cyprus and wasting all that money?' My family and church were all waiting to hear about the day I met my father in Cyprus. The spiritual battle to remain focused on God raged around me.

The day before we were due to return home, I found an information office and picked up a leaflet on an English-speaking evangelical church in Larnaca. The sheen of our foreign trip had worn off. Both Christine and I now felt dejected. Our confidence was further shaken when we were spat at by locals and leered at and approached by drunks. It was the first time we had felt vulnerable as two women travelling alone. I knew that when Satan's territory is encroached upon, snarling, he bares his fangs. He will do anything, however petty, to upset our faith in God and replace it with fear and doubt.

I dreaded the thought of boarding the plane empty-handed. Christine asked John to ring Theo again, but this time he could not get through. Our pleas and enquiries were met with a stony wall of silence.

On our last day in Cyprus, Christine began to feel ill. I went for a walk along the beach alone and cried out to God for my dream. It felt so cruel to come all this way, and see so many amazing colours in God's painting, only to not understand the composition. I felt like a donkey teased by a carrot on a stick. I could taste the dream, but it forever remained out of reach, always one more gruelling step away. I pleaded with my heavenly Father, 'Please, just give me the strength to get back on the plane.'

I sat on the seafront and read from the book of Numbers:

> God is not a man, that he should lie, nor a son of man, that he should change his mind. Does he speak and then not act? Does he promise and not fulfil? (Num. 23:19)

When I returned from my time with God, walking the shifting sands together, Christine felt well enough to attend the evangelical church. It was called Grace Church. The service concentrated on the turning point of human history: the day Jesus defeated Satan and dealt with our sin forever. We heard again the amazing story: despite all that humanity did to the Son of God, his betrayal and humiliation, his torture and crucifixion, he sacrificed his life for us. It was a powerful service that reminded me that anything I thought I was suffering at the hands of God, he had already suffered at the hands of humanity.

I was bruised by the outcome of my Cypriot adventure. Thankfully, the church service was enough to sustain me for the journey home. On the plane, I sat next to a lady who took regular holidays on the island. She asked me what had brought me to the country. I was exhausted and thought, *I can't go through it all right now!* but God gave me the strength. Enthused but tearful, I shared the account of my search. She then told me her own story. Her friend's father had once had an affair, which unbeknown to him produced a child. Years later his mystery daughter tracked him down, boldly declaring her relationship to him. Now they know each other as father and daughter, but they can only meet in hotel rooms. He can only love his daughter secretly because of the shame of his affair.

As soon as I heard this story, I knew that this was not what God wanted for me. I was conceived in secret, and grew up as a secret. I was not about to embark on a clandestine relationship with my own father, waiting for phones to ring in secret hotel rooms. As I sat on the plane, I was hit by the enormity of this revelation. What the girl in the story had done, storming into her father's life, I had told God I didn't want to do. It was for God to turn my father's heart, not me. I had been looking for God's will in Cyprus, and God was building bridges according to his will. Although I was wounded, hearing the woman's story gave me hope. I knew that whenever my reunion would take place, it would be according to God's timing and not mine.

When I returned to England, I shared my encounters with everyone I knew. People were in awe of what had happened, drawing their own conclusions from the events. Was it God or fate, coincidence or luck? My sisters were amazed. Marissa declared that I would never have achieved any of it without my faith. Gemma said that while she had prayed for me, she saw a stone landing in a river and the ripples spreading outwards. I praised God, inspired again as I witnessed the faith around me.

I believed that God would take my separation and turn it into gold. Sometimes as a Christian, I am taken to the limits of my faith, but the prophet Isaiah says in one of his many prophecies of Jesus:

> A bruised reed he will not break, and a smouldering wick he will not snuff out. In faithfulness he will bring forth justice; he will not falter or be discouraged till he establishes justice on earth. In his law the islands will put their hope. (Is. 42:3,4)

I may have been a bruised reed, blown about and lashed by the storm, but I still had a church and a family waiting for me at home. The church was looking to employ a youth pastor, and Tim and I were offered the job of running the youth group. The church leaders knew nothing about us, and believed that they needed to take a step of faith. We had only recently left our old church, Tim had been made redundant, and we were being choked by financial debt. Our CV was not a great one, but Tim was offered the job of youth pastor, and I was to work alongside him.

We needed to relocate to the heart of our church community in Littlehampton. It was an opportunity for the whole family to move on, including Danielle, who was beginning her senior school years. We handed in our notice at our rented Worthing property and moved to Littlehampton to concentrate on settling into church and running the youth evenings.

I shared my vision to search for my father with the church pastor. He did not patronise me, warn me or crush my hope in any way. He listened, stood by me and believed for me. Church had become my home once more and I began to dance again.

20

Mountain Climb

Working for the church allowed me a brief respite from battling for my father. During this time, I sensed God give me a date for when my father would phone me. I told the pastor about this and my friends and family all prayed for this day. However, when I awoke on the morning in question, my heart sank like a stone. I knew without a doubt that I had been mistaken. I had heard God's voice in the past, but not this time.

It left me feeling foolish. But I picked myself up and began to ask God for another opportunity. The very next day, the church pastor phoned to say that he had spoken to Ian McCormack who was about to speak at a church in Cyprus. He asked me whether he could tell Ian about my search, enabling Ian to share my story with the Cypriot pastor. I said yes, faithfully describing the window of opportunity I had prayed for. Perhaps this was it.

I sent Ian a lengthy e-mail explaining the events and details of the last few years. He phoned and we spoke about what to do. I knew Ian was a man who spent his life travelling the world working for God. He would be faithful in doing his best. If he managed to speak to my

161

father, he would bring God's perspective to the situation. I gave him a phone number that I had found through the International Directory Enquiries. I believed it belonged to my father. It was a strange twist in God's plan, that the man whose story had once inspired my vision of Mum, was now engaged in delivering my own story to my father.

In Cyprus, Ian spoke to a church pastor. They were both excited about my story and so they rang my father's contact number, but no such number existed. Ian then put me in direct contact with the pastor. I phoned the Cypriot pastor in the hope that the door was not completely closed. It wasn't. He listened to my story, acknowledging what God was doing. I gave him another number that I had been given by International Directory Enquiries. I believed it belonged to my father's brother, the uncle I had seen sitting in the Cypriot café. It was frustrating stepping back into the exhausting surroundings of the waiting room again; all I could do was reach out in hope. The pastor eventually rang, saying that he had spoken to my uncle's wife. She had sounded genuinely pleased to help and provided the pastor with my father's phone number.

He felt that he needed more time before making the call. I waited for another couple of weeks but it was suffocating me. It felt as if I was being buried under rubble, and every time I picked up the phone to either ask or remind someone, I was clawing my way out one fingernail at a time. The next time I rang the pastor, his enthusiasm had faded. He said that he no longer felt it was his place to get involved. I threw my entire arsenal of 'ifs' and 'buts' at him, willing him to help, but he said that I should ring my father myself.

This was not what I wanted to hear, and so I waited for a couple of days, full of anxiety. I worried that this would soon be another stalemate of endless phone calls and lies. I had been so constricted by lies. I had to free myself from the great lie, but how?

I surrounded myself with prayer. My friend Amanda Hills reminded me that all I was doing was picking up a phone, dialling a number and trying to reach a man who happened to be my father. Although it had never seemed that simple a task, I dialled the number and waited for the ring tone. I asked to speak to Theodoros, but he wasn't there. The number my Cypriot aunt had given the pastor belonged to a record shop. I put the phone down. I was humiliated and hurt.

A couple of days later God told me to ring my uncle, but this had all become a trial. I was aware of the spiritual forces opposed to this reunion and opposed to all the work that God was doing. I remembered hearing how my father didn't want to know me. The subsequent pit of despair had consumed me. Then I remembered asking God that if he could inspire my faith to believe in his promise, then I would never doubt him again. And I knew my faith in God's promise remained.

On God's instruction, I rang my uncle. A woman answered, and I introduced myself, asking whether she spoke English. She said yes, and so without hesitation I said that I was calling from England trying to find my father. She immediately asked whether it was her husband. I explained that it wasn't, but she continued, 'Oh, it would not matter to me if he was. I've always said that if ever something like this should happen, then I would welcome that child into the family with open arms.'

This flood of emotion took me completely by surprise.

'Is it Theo? Is Theo your dad?' she enthused.

'Well, I've heard Theo can help me in finding my dad,' I replied, diplomatically.

Again, she exploded with words. 'If Theo is your dad, then we would welcome you into the family. He's a lovely man.'

She told me that her own father had died when she was a child, and that she would do anything to see him again. I offered cautious replies as I tried to gain some ground in the conversation, but it was like a whirlwind. By the time she had finished talking, I could only reinforce that Theo could help me. I asked whether she had his number, and she asked me to ring back in a couple of weeks.

The number I had rung belonged to my aunt's holiday home. If I had not called on the specific day God instructed me to, then I would not have found her as she was rarely there. I thanked God for his guidance, and although it had not been my father voicing such emotional words of welcome, talking to my aunt had made a refreshing change from previous phone calls. For the first time in my journey, I was hearing extraordinary words of welcome.

My aunt had showered me with wonderful words of encouragement. Every part of me had wanted to say, 'Yes, Theodoros is my dad.' But I held back, giving enough hints only to suggest it. I sat back and prayed while basking in my aunt's talk of open arms. Her words had given new life to a dream that had once been vibrant, but had recently become obscured by dark clouds.

Before ringing my aunt again, I had a dream. I was building a jigsaw puzzle, talking to God while trying to fit the pieces together. The puzzle wasn't a game, and as God spoke to me, his tone was heavy with parental concern. He told me that it was crucial that I put the next piece in place, because if I didn't, then other people could not build around the puzzle. I woke up knowing that I had to make the next move. I had waited for a couple of weeks and now it was time to ring Cyprus again.

When she answered, my aunt said she had spoken to her husband, and she had one question. 'Is Theo your father?'

'Yes,' I said. And then the resistance began.

She asked who had told me, and I said Paul and Nicky, the people Theo had grown up with. I asked if she knew them and she said, 'Yes' but her tone was one of icy hostility. She told me that the people I had spoken to had all lied, including Paul. Theo had not even been in the country during the dates I had given her. She stated that my information was so obviously misguided, that she had not even bothered to contact Theo; it wasn't worth the effort. I was stunned by what she was saying. Was this true? I could hardly speak.

After the phone call, Amanda Hills and I talked about the possibilities. I had no leads left and no plan of action. The search was dwindling as one door after another had closed before me. We prayed about where to go next. Throughout all the setbacks and rejections, prayer was the key. Through prayer I can share the smallest details and the greatest ambitions of my life with God, and he is interested in all of it. I can be honest about my fears, doubts and expectations, and God always listens. Praying to God is like flexing a spiritual muscle; the more often we pray in the name of his Son, the stronger we become in our relationship with our Father. So, I prayed that my father in Cyprus would tell the truth, and that my Father in heaven would demolish this wall of lies.

As Amanda and I prayed, she envisaged a scene where I was standing on top of a mountain. A river flowed down from the mountain, carrying my prayers towards Cyprus. I interpreted this as the power of prayer and God's encouragement to keep praying.

I asked Jesus to let his influence flow over my family. He had once told me that through my testimony, my family would come to me one after the other like waves hitting the shore. I prayed that I would not be beaten back by fear, but I would wait for God to shatter the rock which had separated my family.

Once again I was stirred into action. I phoned my aunt again, not really knowing what to say. She immediately blasted into her frantic claims that Theo wasn't my father, all the dates were wrong.

I challenged her. 'If Theo is not my father, then all those years ago when I wrote him a letter, why didn't he write back telling me I was mistaken? If he had nothing to hide, then when I visited Cyprus, and he knew the hotel I was staying in, why didn't he come and tell me that the dates were wrong? Why didn't he clear himself when he had the chance?'

She became hesitant and then desperate, trying to push the conversation away from my questions. Eventually my aunt told me to let go of my father.

'The best thing for you to do,' she said, 'is to pretend that he is dead.'

And there stands the wisdom of the world. But I stood against it and declared that I would never give up. Our conversation ended, but I knew that God would break the lies the world cowers behind, because to him, all human wisdom is foolishness. I realised how far I had come. I had developed a new confidence, and just one remark was not going to deter me.

My father had received letters and photographs; old friends such as Nicky had contacted him regarding the matter. He knew I had travelled personally to his home village, and he had chosen to hide. Now, as I had infiltrated his very family, the net must have felt tighter than ever. The army that raged between us was scheming to cut this line of communication. But my heavenly Father was unfolding his plans for the future of my family. I knew that I was Theo's daughter, and I was not about to pretend he was dead. God, not the world, would have the final word on the matter.

I had recently met a lady at church called Pip Smith. We became friends and I found out that she was joining a team who were travelling to Switzerland. They had plans to pray on top of a mountain. As soon as I heard this, I felt my spirit leap inside me, and I told her about what Amanda Hills had prayed. As I shared my concerns with God, I heard him say, 'Go to Switzerland.'

The lady leading the trip was called Jo Thatcher. She was the pastor's sister-in-law and the mother of four teenage daughters, one of whom was a member of our youth group. I saw Jo one day and told her about Amanda Hill's picture. I also told her about God's instruction. Jo invited me to accompany her team to Switzerland.

I didn't know a lot about Jo, but I had met her late husband, John. He had been one of the church leaders. John had encouraged Tim and me when we first arrived at Arun. Not long after we joined, the church received some devastating news. While climbing a mountain in Switzerland, John had suffered a heart attack. He had collapsed and died on the mountain slope. Arun Community Church had lost one of its pivotal leaders and responded by drawing closer to God, hungry to understand the purpose behind John's apparently senseless departure. I watched Jo and her daughters' devastation in the face of such enormous loss. We seldom understand the timing and meaning of events such as these, but can find comfort in recognising that even death is under God's control. It is never an accident. Through the devastation, Jo would inherit her husband's heart and passion for Switzerland.

Jo wanted to go to Switzerland to see what God had prepared for her. I understood the importance of her finding that purpose for her life, as I had made my own journey to Cyprus. God had widened my vision for Cyprus, and now my search had taken a completely unexpected turn. It had been interwoven with Jo's passion for Switzerland. I was about to learn from Jo what it really meant to believe and pray for a nation.

The valley where Jo's husband died is known as 'The Rooftop of Europe'. The mountains are not the highest in Europe but the valley is the highest valley floor. Therefore many believe it is a spiritual battlefield of some significance because it is the 'High Place of Europe'. Many others come to this place – some to support the Christian work in the area and others to set themselves up in opposition and set up altars to their gods and to take spiritual ground. Our little team of Jo, me and our friend Pip Smith joined some Swiss friends in an attempt to get to the top. The mountain is significant because at the very summit is located the main source of three of Europe's major rivers. This is called 'Die Dreieinigkeit Europas' (The Trinity of Europe). The rivers rise up on the summit of this mountain. They are no more than bubbling puddles at this stage but a concrete marker has been set up over the spot and we planned to pray, speak out the Word of God, and pour oil, salt, wine, bread, water into the source.

On the way up the mountain we saw many shrines to other gods had been built, including a face with a five-pointed star in the middle of its forehead. Through prayer we demolished every one we found and asked the Lord to receive back this place. We believed that something powerful happened that day so that the Lord's love and freedom cry could flow out to all parts of Europe.

This wasn't the only powerful thing that was occurring. The Lord was breaking down barriers in my path too. Just as Amanda Hills had foreseen, one of those rivers flows south into the Adriatic, part of the Mediterranean and eventually reaches the shores of Cyprus.

There was a lot of fear in me on the day of the climb. I wasn't very fit, and I had never attempted anything like it before. The air was so thin that my throat burned, and I prayed that God would give me the physical strength to accomplish the mission. It became a repeat of when I first gave my life to him, when he had almost carried me to the front of the hall. Now I was reaching another landmark. I screamed out against all the frustrating years of searching for my father. I asked God that if the path I had trodden had not been his will, then could he remove the spiritual ache of my desire. With every step, I recommitted my life to walking for God and not myself.

I read from the Gospel of Matthew:

> You are the light of the world. A city on a hill cannot be hidden. (Mt. 5:14)

God encouraged me, 'Forget the hill, I have put you on a mountain.'

I cried because the last person who had spoken into this situation had been my aunt, telling me that Theo wasn't my father. Every time I absorbed such attacks, I felt hidden again, just as my mum had once pushed me down out of sight. When I heard God confirm that he had brought me to this place, I felt his pride in me for sticking with him. Armed with the Word of God, we prayed over Europe from the high ground. It was a breathtaking experience.

On the way down, we stopped at a lake, where we took communion together. After I had taken the wine and the bread the Holy Spirit hit me like a bolt of lightning. To anyone watching it must have looked like I was having a fit, because my body shook and convulsed as I was thrown onto the floor. The others prayed over me – I was coming into a new covenant with God my Father. God had written a new contract for me. I had prayed that I would not return from the mountain the same person.

Jo poured the wine into the lake. We watched as the red wine fanned out and was taken into the waters to begin its long journey across Europe. We prayed for the millions that lived along the shores of these rivers, part of which had been hidden behind an iron curtain of silence for half a century. We prayed that the silence would be broken and for a great change to come across Europe. The barriers of silence were being broken in the heavens and God was about to bring things that were hidden out into the light. Jo, too, had asked God for change. I knew that by acknowledging the sacrifice of her husband John, she had accepted a momentous calling on her life.

I had gone to Switzerland with no real hope – with only negative words resounding in my ears. But God was restoring my faith in the things that were happening in heaven, in the things I could not see. Barriers were indeed being removed. Both Jo and I came down the mountain changed people.

21

Royal Sword

It was a complete surprise. Amanda Hills rang me one day, saying that she believed I needed to ring Stelios, my sister Lynn's father. It led me back into prayer to find God's will. I read through my diary, revisiting my battle with Lynn's uncle, Paul. God promised that I would know my father's name in a couple of days, and right on cue, an unsuspecting Paul gave up the name 'Theodoros'. My aunt had recently accused all the people in England of lying, denouncing all my information as flawed. My diary reminded me that this very information had come from God. He knew that my hope would be shattered by my aunt's denial. In times of such attacks against his plan, God had planted evidence of his absolute control that stirred my faith and spurred me on.

Years ago, when I wrote my first letter to my father, Lynn asked me to pass on Stelios's number in the hope that Theo would get in touch with him. Having asked God that it was right to ring Stelios myself, I made the call to Australia. A man answered the phone; I introduced myself as Pam's daughter Mandy Curtis, because that was how Stelios would have known me. I asked if his name was Stelios and whether he remembered my mother. He said, 'Yes.'

He sounded surprised and uneasy, so I grabbed the opportunity to confirm whether Theodoros Antonios Selios was my father's name. Again he said, 'Yes.'

'Are there people in the background making it hard for you to talk?' I asked.

'Yes.'

The nature of this conversation was the opposite of my aunt's endless chatter, and it made life a lot easier for me. All Stelios had to do was listen, and so I told him that Lynn had tried looking for him, but she had stopped because she didn't want to upset his family.

'Lynn wrote a letter to you once. Not a day goes by when she doesn't think about you,' I said.

Stelios said, 'Me too.'

I challenged him. 'Are you saying, that there's not a day that goes by when you don't think about your daughter Lynn?'

'Yes.' It struck me that despite whoever might be listening, he had still wanted to communicate his loss. I left him with Lynn's phone number and pleaded with him to contact her. He said that he would. I pray that he will. Life is too short to miss such opportunities for reconciliation.

We need our relationships as parents and as children. They are physical and spiritual and God designed the human race to function this way. The pool I had waded through in search of my father was stirred up again. It might have settled, but God was not allowing it to stagnate. I asked God where to go, because I had called every number and chased every available lead.

The very next day, a friend of mine sent me a card. She said that while praying, she had seen me standing in a dry and rocky place. Although I thought I was lost, God wanted me to know that I was where he wanted me to be. From out of the rocks above would come a waterfall. I was standing where streams of living water were preparing to flow. She gave me a passage from the book of Isaiah. It read:

> The poor and needy search for water, but there is none; their tongues are parched with thirst. But I the LORD will answer them . . . I will make rivers flow on barren heights . . . I will turn the desert into pools of water, and the parched ground into springs. (Is. 41:17,18)

It was nearing the end of 2003 and I attended a local prayer meeting. During the meeting, one of the guests prayed that God would restore to me everything I had lost. She confirmed that I would meet my father, and encouraged me by saying that although my walk was hard, it was because I had to become who God wanted me to be. She also confirmed that God was working on my father's heart, telling Theo not to worry because everything would be well. After the meeting I felt as though God was holding me above Satan's bed of lies. He was building a bridge that would reach over to my father. I believed that when Theo looked out across the bridge, God would prompt him to take his first steps towards his daughter.

Tim's brother, Simon, had been collecting and writing Christian testimonies. We had written a short account of my story and for a long time I had felt I should write a book about my life. God said that I was to start the book now, and that by the end of the book I would have met my father. I told Simon that we should take my testimony and expand it into a book and so, together with Gemma, who was now his wife, we prayed for my father. We asked God to break Theo free from the mindset of the world, to break off the lies that were holding him back. We prayed for the book, and I had a strong feeling that before we had even begun, Simon needed to return home and write the last chapter. He needed to write the account of me meeting my father, because I believed it would be prophetic.

When we prophesy, we speak out what is on God's heart; it can be the foretelling of God's desire for the future; it can also apply to either the past or the present. Some people see pictures when they pray, and these pictures can be prophetic illustrations of God's desire.

The following day, I held my 2004 diary before God. As I did this, I believe that God said it would be the year in which my father and I would meet. At the Wednesday night youth meeting, I received further confirmation that God was changing my father's attitude towards me. A few days later I phoned Simon and to my delight he had written about the meeting between my father and me. On 31 November 2003, this is what he wrote:

I sat down with the man who I knew to be my father, but the father I had never known. His eyes were glazed, tired, somewhat distracted – maybe even afraid. He had known of my existence solely from my persistence in searching him out. I was the daughter and woman who had invaded his life and marched her way towards him. He knew of this. He knew that I had toppled obstacles as strategic as chess pieces to reach him. And in our different ways, we were both already exhausted – and yet no word had been spoken. I was exhausted from the pursuit, and he in his shabby dignity, was exhausted from running.

I smiled at what had been an impossible journey, full of pain and doubt, people and opinions. Could God have carried me through a dryer and more fearful wilderness, a more desolate arena, scorched by the sheer bleakness of it all, but always overcast with clouds of promise. He had sat me in front of my father, but my thoughts were of God, and the risk he had run in delivering me to a man that I had dreamt of since childhood. God could have kept me for himself, but he carried me here. I felt the peace of his presence, as I began a relationship that had taken 32 years to begin, but was eternal in its design. As I took my father's hand, God's love for this man was unleashed.

I read about my feelings and my father's feelings, but most important were the words: 'I began a relationship that had taken 32 years to begin, but was eternal in its design.' Simon admitted that he had not wanted to write what he thought I wanted to read. I now had two words, one saying I would meet my father in 2004, the other stating that I would be thirty-two, which could lead the search into 2005. Both followed God's infallible promise that I would meet my father. Surely now my search was nearing its end.

As Simon and I were about to begin the book, a friend from the prayer meeting told me that God had given her a picture of my heart, which was covered in writing. Through this illustration, she claimed that God had already written the book on my heart. I was pointed towards the book of Revelation, where it says:

> He who was seated on the throne said, 'I am making everything new!' Then he said, 'Write this down, for these words are trustworthy and true.' (Rev. 21:5)

God told me that the book was going to be a spearhead, the point of which would puncture the lies that have been spoken about him. He was going to arm me with a mighty weapon.

Every New Year's Day, I meet with my sisters. Sometimes it's a painful reunion. Each annual occasion reminds us of what the family has lost. At the beginning of 2004 my sister Bev told me that Alan, one of my childhood neighbours, had died through an illness related to heroin addiction. Simon and I had already begun discussing the book. He needed a beginning, and so we decided to visit the town where I'd grown up. We drove over one morning, arrived at the green and agreed to visit Alan's mother. I knocked on the door of the old terraced house that stood next door to the house I grew up in. Alan's mum was surprised to see me, and she invited us both in for a cup of tea.

She described the harrowing effects heroin had wreaked on her son's mental and physical state. I could see for myself the strain it had put on her family. Alan's mum showed us photographs from the 1970s, in which Alan and I stood together in washed-out colours on the communal green. As I revisited these faded memories, I asked God for the right words.

Alan's mum knew me as the girl who had played with her sons, but she knew nothing of the abuse I had suffered. I began to talk to her about these painful parts of my testimony, a little of what brought me to the point in my bedroom when I cried out to God.

After listening to my story, Alan's mum confessed, 'You know what, Alan started going to church before he died, he had found peace there, and in the hospital he told me that he was never going to touch heroin again. He had said this hundreds of times before and gone back on his word. But this time he was different and I believed him. For a moment it was like having my son back.'

I showed Simon around my childhood town. We looked for my name which I had once engraved on a bench, and we saw the old sweet shop where I spent Paul's money. Now it stood empty and boarded up. I visited my old school where the gangs marked their territories in the playground, and where bitter differences were fought out in the fields. We found the bungalow where I used to smoke Mary's cigarettes, and the brick area where her husband had raped one of the local girls. Mary had died long ago.

We left these frayed edges behind and returned to Littlehampton. In the town where I'd grown up lay a dark past where seeds were planted which years later took me to the edge of suicide. But my life was different now, and although parts of my past remained painful, God had set me free to grow into his future.

I returned to church with the conviction that the writing of my story was to be done now, despite it having no ending. At a church thanksgiving service I offered my life back to God, and as I did, I knew that God wanted everything. He wanted my story: he wanted me to give back to him every detail, to talk about my family, the abortions, the abuse and rape. God wanted everything that had been kept private and hidden.

I love God, and he comes first in my life, but my major weakness is in wanting to be loved by people. I know that a lot of my past exploits do not paint me in an attractive light. I made a lot of choices that were wrong, but God has forgiven me for all of them. As I stood at the front of the church, I also stood in the confidence that God would protect me throughout the anticipated exposure.

The previous year, before my birthday in 2003, Tim's brother Simon woke up one morning with a vivid picture in his mind. He saw a finely crafted and engraved silver pen being lovingly put back into its gift case. It was like a royal sword being returned to its scabbard at the end of a victorious battle. Then he saw my face reflecting the fulfilment of whatever the pen had written. It would take almost a year for God to reveal the meaning of this image.

Together with Simon, I began to fashion the spearhead for God's assault. I spoke into a Dictaphone, sometimes discovering memories as I narrated my past. Simon took the recorded material away to compose as a story. We prayed about God's plan for the book, asking that his testimony would be like spiritual dynamite in the hands of the abused, the depressed, the lonely, the bullied, the bereaved, those caught in addictions, destructive habits and broken relationships, especially with their parents. We wanted God to speak to those who are hungry for a deeper relationship with him, to call back those who have fallen away, and to reach out to the people who have never known Jesus. We had no ending and no deadline, but we were armed with God's promise that I would one day meet my father.

Part IV

The Promised Land

Part IV

The Promised Land

22

Jericho Walls

Wild drumming and Middle Eastern chants punctuated the breath-taking scenes before me. It was April 2004, and I was watching Mel Gibson's controversial block-buster, *The Passion of the Christ*. As I saw this artistic account of the last hours of Jesus' life, I was reminded again of what Christ went through. I watched the violent moments of humiliation and torture, as Jesus gave up his own power and reputation to die for us all.

I was astonished to return to see the film again, this time with Andy, Danielle's father, much to the shock of his friends and family. We watched it in silence, and after the film had finished, I said to Andy, 'Look at what God gave up for you. He raised people from the dead, he healed the sick, people fell at his feet in worship, and yet he gave up his reputation and died for you. Will you give up your reputation for him?'

The year before, Andy had been arrested. While waiting for the court's decision, the reality of prison cast its ugly shadow over the family. The case was called and then adjourned, and over the ensuing months, I prayed with friends and family that God was in control. In his state of self-preservation, Andy consistently told his solicitors that he was not guilty. Every time I saw Danielle struggling with the thought of her father locked up in a prison cell, I prayed that God would prompt Andy to tell the truth.

On the day that Andy was due in court, Danielle stayed home from school waiting to hear news of the verdict. Despite what he was telling his solicitors, I knew that Andy was guilty. If he went to prison, I didn't want Danielle believing that either God or the law was in the wrong. I prayed that Danielle would be open to however God chose to answer our prayers. Later that day I spoke to Andy on the phone. His solicitors had informed him that if he pleaded not guilty, he would go to prison for eight years. In the courtroom Andy finally told the truth and his sentence was postponed to a later date.

I praised God that the truth was out. If Andy had stood in court and lied, he would have gone to prison. Andy had shown that he was now willing to admit to his actions and accept the consequences. What he didn't know was that God himself had seen this change. There was still the threat of a three-year prison sentence. But I could not believe that while I was waiting for a reunion with my father, God would take Danielle's away. Andy had been given another chance. The final court appearance at which Andy would be sentenced was scheduled for April 2004. I began to talk seriously with him about his chosen path, asking him why he didn't want more from his life. His answer was that he hated himself, and it broke my heart to hear this. I knew that while Andy turned his frustration on himself, accepting his drinking and depression, Jesus was waiting to breathe life into him. I knew the path Andy had walked; I knew exactly what Jesus wanted to save him from.

Throughout this saga, Danielle and I were brought closer. There were moments when she needed to cry out to God for her own father. My friend, Amanda Hills, gave me a scripture for Danielle from the book of Esther. Esther had been made Queen and was asked by King Xerxes:

> What is it, Queen Esther? What is your request? Even up to half the kingdom, it will be given you. (Esth. 5:3)

I told Danielle that she now had to ask God for exactly what she wanted. Danielle asked for two things. The first was that her father would not go to prison. The second was that he would give up an existence soaked in drinking and depression for a life with Jesus.

It dawned on me that Andy didn't know about my abuse and rape. I began to tell him, mainly to illustrate that I was unhappy before I had met him. Therefore, my misery had not been solely his fault. We were talking on the phone the day before his final court appearance, and God prompted me to give him a very early draft of the book. When he came to collect Danielle later that day, I handed him a copy of the book, but every part of me wanted to run after him and snatch it back to safety. I was terrified, knowing the honesty I had applied in describing our relationship.

On the day of Andy's sentence, I sent him a text message. It said that now he had told the truth, God was going to work. God's mercy triumphs over judgement, and in Andy's case judgement could mean a prison sentence, but God's mercy is stronger. Andy stood in court and once again the family waited for the verdict. He phoned later that day to say that he had received two years' probation; he was not going to prison. I thanked God for his mercy, but in the middle of my praises, Andy told me that he had read the book. My heart froze. Tim and I had invited him over for dinner later that evening, and Andy said he would talk to me about it then.

When I drove over to Worthing to collect him, he handed me the manuscript.

'You've read it, then?' I asked, tentatively.

Andy looked at me and said, 'I was up all night reading it. I've read it twice.' I saw the tears in his eyes as he added, 'I'm sorry.'

I couldn't believe he was apologising, and although I didn't need to hear it, it was amazing that he needed to say it. I asked him whether he remembered the events in the book, and he said that it had taken the book to remind him. Years of alcohol and drug abuse had helped to erode any clear account of his past. However, he did speak shamefully about the insults and threats that he had thrown at me. I had expected anger over my perspective of our past and his family. He questioned the relevance of dragging up such memories. I explained that the book was not about attacking anyone, but to tell the story of how God saved me.

That night, Andy joined me, Tim and Danielle for dinner. It was a light celebration of relief, and when the evening was over, I drove Andy home. He was in a reflective mood, and he admitted, 'I've been swimming around with the sharks for too long now, and it's about time that I started swimming in the other direction.'

In the book of Isaiah, the prophet speaks of God bringing change:

> I will lead the blind by ways they have not known, along unfamiliar paths I will guide them; I will turn the darkness into light before them and make the rough places smooth. These are the things I will do; I will not forsake them. (Is. 42:16)

Andy himself was now declaring his desire to change. He may not have gone to prison because of his daughter's prayers, but Andy was still a prisoner of his self-hatred, as I had once been to mine. I knew that Andy's hard-man reputation was standing between him and God. I also knew that God wouldn't only honour half of his promise to Danielle. He sees Andy being carried by the tide, stranded out at sea, and he is committed to bringing him home. Jesus shed his blood for this broken man, and he wants to save him, and others like him, from the dead, black eyes and blood-stained teeth of the sharks.

I am grateful for the father that Andy has been to Danielle. He has not been the perfect parent, but neither have I. Only God can truly fulfil that role. However, Andy has always remained faithful to his daughter. I thank God that since Andy and I separated, and as Tim and I have built a family together, Andy has not walked away from Danielle. We have all made the most of providing Danielle with the love that a daughter needs. There have been times when it has been hard for her, not having her father around, but she knows that he is only a phone call away.

Before the summer of 2004 I had a dream. It ran like a set of instructions in which I believe God told me to ring International Directory Enquiries again, and that they would give me a new number, which would be 'the right one'. The following morning I carried out the directions from the dream. I rang Directory Enquiries and asked for the phone number of Theodoros Antonios Selios. As depicted in the dream, they supplied me with a new number and so I wrote it down in a notepad. I rang it but it did not exist. Tim rang it to make sure there was no mistake. Each time we were told that number was not

available. In this case I decided that the dream had defi-
nitely not been from God.

Not wanting to delay the progress of the book, I
forged ahead with it. It was being declared on paper that
I would meet my father soon. It was as though the very
writing of the book had become like the walls of Jericho.

In the book of Joshua, Moses' successor, we read in
chapter 6 that the city of Jericho barricaded itself from
the Israelite army. God instructed Joshua to march the
armed men around the city walls daily for six days. On
the seventh day, he was told to march the Israelite army
around the city seven times. At the final blast of the
priests' trumpets, the army shouted its battle cry and the
walls of Jericho fell. God delivered the city to his people.
In the story, God gave detailed instructions regarding
what he wanted the Israelites to do in order for the city
to fall. He could have smashed down the walls in an
instant, but he chose to work with his people. They
marched in faith and obedience, and he provided the
power from heaven. God can break down the obstacles
in all our lives, but he gives the victory to those who
obey him. Regarding the writing of the book, I knew that
I needed to be obedient to everything God said.

On reflection, there have been times when I have not
understood this journey. I remembered my frustration in
Cyprus. Expecting celebration, instead I had to share my
rejection with a stranger on the plane home. These were
lessons in obedience that God needed me to walk
through. If writing this book was marching around
Satan's walls, I needed to follow God's instructions to
prepare the way for his miracle. As God's promises were
written down, Satan's obstructions were being challenged. This was spiritual warfare.

My regular prayer group prayed week after week for
my reunion. During one such meeting, it was spoken of

how the miracle would not happen until the eleventh hour. I feared having to wait until Christmas, but God added to this message. I saw the book, a pen, and a full stop being put into place. He reassured me that I need not worry, because when the full stop was reached and nothing more could be written, the pen would not have time to be put back into its case. It would be picked up again to write the final chapter. Like the walls of Jericho, the details of the book were completely under God's timing and control.

My sister Carol was due to visit my home in Littlehampton. I was looking forward to spending time with her, because as a child I had always been close to Carol. Unfortunately, our relationship had suffered over a disagreement following my conversion to Christianity. I woke up on the morning of Carol's visit, prompted by the Holy Spirit to give her a copy of the unfinished book. I paced up and down nervously. Along with personal family details, the book also contained a large amount of spiritual material, and I was not sure how my family would react to this. I had included my vision of Mum, given to me not through the mysticism of a medium, but as I believed and had claimed, by God himself.

It was a fierce battle to accept that I should even consider giving Carol a copy. I picked up the manuscript from the bedroom and I was physically shaking as I walked downstairs. I handed it to Carol and told her that I was shaking because I was so nervous. Carol was puzzled. 'Why, Mand? Why do you feel like that?'

I had to be honest. 'It's because I fear upsetting the family and I fear rejection.'

As Carol left, I asked her to contact me because I would not rest until I knew what she thought. Carol smiled and offered me her reassurance.

'It doesn't matter what you've said. I won't reject you.'

A couple of days later I received a phone call. It was Carol. She had read the book, and began to speak about some of the incidents in my past. As we talked about these details, it helped to heal our relationship, and my sister also felt able to talk about her own father. When Carol was thirteen, Mum had announced that her father was coming to the house to see her. Up until this point in time, Carol had never met him. They met briefly and then he disappeared again. Years later, when she was married, Carol traced her father and arranged to meet him. It transpired that for years he had passed her in the street and even sat near her in the same pub. Carol had never been aware of this, but Mum had. Carol met her father again and gained a new family, but everything turned sour when a DNA test was requested. While her father had confessed to a one-night stand with Mum, Mum's reputation for sleeping around was used to challenge whether Carol was actually his. In anger, Carol declined the test. She knew that he was her father, and so did he. They both knew his affair had been much more than the one night, but he had chosen to keep this a secret. The dream ended for Carol. The relationship faded away.

When Carol read about my search for my father, she did not dismiss my hopes or faith. Her concern was a sisterly, 'What if it doesn't happen?' I understood her viewpoint. She had read an unfinished book building up to an event that could be written off as pure fantasy, and based on her own experiences, could lead to further heartache. I could only pray for God to unveil his plans for my family.

23

Jigsaw Puzzle

The crowds numbered thousands. It was a Christian youth festival called 'Soul Survivor'. In the summer of 2004, Tim and I took the church's older youth there. We packed our tents – and being in England, our winter clothes (!) – entrusting Simon and Gemma with Ethan and Joseph for the week. The boys were keen for us to go, holding on to a promised trip to Legoland on our return. The previous year, Tim had taken the youth by himself, and I had stayed home with the boys, Danielle and her cousin Sian. This time both girls came with us. Leaving Danielle behind was not an option, as she had become a little sister to the youth group. We knew they would look after her.

When we arrived at the festival, I was worried for Sian. This was not a relaxed *Songs of Praise* service with hymn sheets and sweet choir singing. At Soul Survivor, people lay flat out on the floor, after experiencing what they believe is the overwhelming presence of God's Spirit. People cried in worship, and shook uncontrollably as they raised their hands. They called out in strange languages, believing this to be a gift from the Holy Spirit. I'd taken Sian to Arun Community Church

189

before, but the atmosphere here was more intense – and on a bigger scale. I worried what my sister Lynn would think if her daughter returned home traumatised! I prayed.

During the very first meeting the worship was lifted to heaven. There was a physical presence of the Holy Spirit moving among the crowd. As I sang and prayed, I had a now familiar picture of myself standing on mountaintops. This time the mountains became smaller as I was lifted above them. They looked like peaks and contours drawn on a map. As I saw these mountains beneath me, I sensed that God was saying to look over this map from his perspective. All of a sudden, I 'saw' Carol, Lynn, and all my sisters praising God. And I realised that Sian would go home full of excitement, buzzing – she'd be a witness for all she'd seen. Then I remembered the card my friend had sent to me, describing how I was standing in a dry place. Cracks were forming in the rocks above, and God's living water was going to pour through. God reminded me that the dam had been broken, and his power was about to fall on my family.

On day three of the event, I passed a tent where a seminar on prophecy was about to start. The endless rain and mud had given me a craving for a hot chocolate, and so I found a drink and sat down in the meeting.

I listened to the speaker. His teaching was good, although it was aimed at a younger audience. At the end of the meeting, he asked us to split into groups of three to pray with one another. I stood with a young girl and an older man who I thought was possibly her father. The idea of the exercise was not to ask anything about each other, but to allow the Holy Spirit alone to guide our prayers. It would be a step of faith. As they prayed for me, I wanted to tell the girl that one day she was going to meet her father. I tried to reason that she might in fact be standing next to her father, in which case my prayer would sound completely stupid.

As I began to pray, all I could hear were the words, 'Tell her that one day she is going to meet her father.' The need to say this grew stronger, like heat being turned to a much higher temperature. I said to the girl, 'Look, I don't know you, but I feel that God wants you to know that one day you are going to meet your father.'

She burst into tears and, as I continued to pray, I could tell that God was speaking to her. She had not realised how much she needed to hear God's revelation, any more than I had, five years ago. I saw reflections of myself in the tears of this weeping girl, and when we stopped praying, I asked her about her life. She had never met her father, and her mother had never told him about her. There was an instant connection between us, and I shared my own story with this young girl.

In the book of Malachi, the prophet states that in the last days, God is going to restore the family. He is going to turn the hearts of fathers towards their children, and the hearts of children towards their fathers (see Mal. 4:6). This was happening before my very eyes. God was turning this girl's heart towards the father she had never met. Thanks to the heart of God, she was about to begin her own story, her own search. Perhaps one day she would write her own book.

My niece, Sian, had been affected by the festival; this I knew had much wider implications for the rest of my family. The dams had broken.

It was Danielle's thirteenth birthday, and my sister Lynn came over from Eastbourne. Before she left, Lynn and I watched one of my favourite films, *Good Will Hunting*. There is a scene in the film when the counsellor (played by Robin Williams), breaks through Matt Damon's character's façade. He thinks that his abusive upbringing has left him unaffected, but his walls of self-persecution are shattered as he is told that the pain he carries is not his fault. It is a powerful moment between the two characters, and I cannot watch it without crying. It was the first time Lynn had watched the film, and I saw her wipe away a few tears of her own. When the film was over, I told her, 'I've almost finished my book.'

'What book?' she asked, thinking I meant a book I was reading.

I told her that it was a book about my life, and because it covered my abuse, I was prepared to change the names of people and places if necessary. I asked Lynn whether she knew that my uncle had abused me, and her answer was astonishing.

'Well, Mand, he did it to me and another sister too. The family knew, but nothing was ever done about it. In fact, quite a few of Mum's boyfriends also abused us.' Lynn concluded, 'That's why I am what I am. That's why I can't ever have a man living in my house or around my children. That's why I can't ever have a relationship with a man. I can't trust them.'

As I listened to Lynn, it was like listening to an echo of Mum. I remembered Lynn once crying in her father's arms in Mum's hallway. When I'd asked Mum what the matter was, she'd said coldly that Lynn's father, Stelios, was moving to Australia, and Lynn would never see him again. In my young mind, I could not grasp why it had to be so final, and so I asked Mum if they could write to each other.

'It's too dangerous, Mand,' she replied. 'The family might find out.'

I remembered my pain and upset as I watched Stelios leave. Mum had built walls around her emotions, and neither her daughters nor their fathers were allowed beyond her defences. She had denied herself the free-dom to love us.

When Lynn told me of her own abuse we held hands and cried. I knew Lynn could not recognise the extent of her pain. She had her own dark room, just as I had had, but it had taken the strong hand of God to lead me through mine. As Lynn held my hand she said, 'You know what? We'll go to Cyprus one day.'

I told her that I would love to do that. When I had travelled to Cyprus with Christine Beales, Lynn claimed that I was mad to look for my father. Ever since then, I had guarded my story from her. Now I felt it was right to tell her the truth.

'Do you know the reason I couldn't take you to Cyprus?'

She assumed that the trip had been arranged on such short notice that it had left me with no time to ask her.

I said, 'No. It was because I needed to pray in Cyprus, and I didn't want to put that weight on your shoulders. You'll understand when you read the book.'

I gave her a copy, knowing that God was reaching out his hand to my eldest sister.

On 9 September, I attended a women's meeting. Over one hundred women from the church met together to attend the weekend events, which included teaching, prayer and a chance to socialise away from the children. After the Saturday teaching, I sat on Littlehampton beach with my friend Amanda Hills.

We sat together watching the sea, and praying. Amanda said that she had seen the pages of a book being flicked through, before the book was finally closed. She then saw a child being lifted onto its father's shoulders. I sensed that I was not to worry. All I needed to do was let God carry me through these final stages of waiting. I prayed for my father and I felt my faith swell within me.

On the Sunday morning in church, the presence of God was rich and intimate. I looked up at the ceiling, and because the church is held in a school sports hall, the roof is a grid of metal. Among a handful of wedged basketballs, I could see a yellow shuttlecock resting on one of the latticed girders. No event, however seemingly insignificant, is out of God's range. He spoke to me through this image of the shuttlecock.

'All it takes,' he said, 'is a gust of wind, and that object will fall. And all it takes is a breath of my Spirit for your father to change his thinking and come to you.'

Perhaps God would place Theo in the throes of indecision. And when the time came for him to fall, God would be poised to catch him.

That morning, I fell on my knees in praise. A lady who knew nothing of my situation prayed for me. She said that God gave her a picture of a jigsaw puzzle, and he wanted me to know that the last piece was about to be put into place. I cried tears of joy when I heard this because I had last seen this image in a dream. I remembered God guiding me through the battle with my Cypriot aunt. He had spoken of the importance of placing the next piece of the puzzle, because without my obedience, people could not build around his vision. Now he was completing the broken picture.

Another lady who I didn't know also asked to pray for me. She said that there had been a carrot on a stick dangling in front of me, leading the way. Now it was time to take it, because God does not lead people on in false hope. Again, this was such a personal picture, because the carrot image was from my trip to Cyprus. Before returning home empty-handed, I had cried to

God on the Greek sands about how bitter the rejection tasted. I felt like a donkey teased by an elusive reward.

I contacted my old friend Christine Beales to update her on everything that God was doing. We had not seen each other recently but Christine remained the same gentle spirit who saw me through my early days of Christian healing. I explained to her what God was unleashing, and together we shared our prayers of celebration. Christine had been praying for the book that very morning. She believed that the book was going to be a spearhead into dark places. From shuttlecocks to jigsaw puzzles, from carrots to spearheads, I was reminded of all the pieces of my journey! I felt as if God was carrying me on his shoulders because all around me the tidal waters were rising. I could see the swelling of the waves, moving in to wash over my parched and scattered family.

I had been inspired by a vision of myself standing on a bridge. My hands were raised to heaven and Mum was standing beside me. Behind me were my friends and family, the people who stepped forward to believe and encourage me on my journey. My father stood in front of me with his wife; she was supporting his decision. Behind them, their family was gathered. God had called everybody together to witness the reunion on the bridge he had built. As the two sides met, God spoke the words, 'Those who put their trust in me, will never be put to shame.'

I also believed this amazing reunion would begin by meeting my father in a café. After we had spoken, I saw myself handing him a copy of the book. It could be the act of reading this very book, raw and unpublished, that would help to take our relationship beyond that first meeting.

If this search and the accompanying book were not God's will, then it would be a waste of time. Without it being part of God's plan it would mean nothing, because the glory would not go to him. It was possible that I could accomplish the act of meeting my father by perseverance alone; I could march into Larnaca, recruit my old friend John the taxi driver, and knock on my father's door. It would be a fascinating human-interest story, celebrating one woman's determination and grit. Perhaps I would be applauded on daytime television for overcoming impossible odds. But the truth was, that from its inception this had always been *God's* story. Not only did he want to bring my father to me, but he also wanted to heal my family and set them free from a pattern of destruction.

When my search took me to Cyprus, I secretly dreaded the first conversation with my father revolving around the subject of God. This was because I feared I might frighten him away and lose him again. I could only imagine how overwhelming it might be for my father to be given a book written about him!

When I first became a Christian, I was given a few simple words written on a slip of paper. They described how God would bless me for choosing to walk with him. That has happened. And I knew that one day, Theo would read of God's love for him, unleashed, as he chose to step on to the bridge to meet his daughter.

24

Full Stop

It was a reminder of God's hand hovering over every detail of my journey. In November 2004 I found an old diary that dated back to 2002. As I flicked through the pages I stopped at 29 July where I had written:

> God is building me up and I feel as if something is going to happen. I think God has given me a title for a book 'Search for a Father'. I will write a book one day and before I begin I will know the ending.

As I settled into November, I remembered what somebody had said about 'the eleventh hour' and so I began to prepare to meet my father. But as the year drew to a close, my expectancy crumbled. Making such declarations about my father had become increasingly difficult. Each time I spoke about it being a promise from God, I was left floundering. It was time to arrange a prayer meeting.

I wanted to bring together everyone who had remained with me throughout my search. Before the meeting I walked along the beach. I asked God to strip away the poisonous doubts that had smothered me like ivy. I knew that underneath I was healthy and strong. I wanted to remain focused on all that God had done, and not be distracted from it.

The group gathered, and that evening we all prayed, believing that God had called my father and that it would take all our prayers to reel him in. We remembered my father's name, meaning 'Gift from God'. And we prayed that God would breathe his Spirit into my father's heart, and wake him from his fear and denial. It was as if the enemy camp had stood for so long, it would take a heavenly army to march in and rescue him from its clutches.

As I sat at home one December night watching a film, without even thinking about my father the word 'tomorrow' filled my mind. I asked God silently, 'Are you saying that it is going to happen tomorrow? Because if so, then could you protect my mind from deception so that I know I've heard from you?'

That night I dreamt about my father. He was turning towards me as I held his face gently in my hands. I woke up at least three times, drifting and then waking. Each time I was filled with the relief that this was from God and that I had not been deceived. I asked him whether there was anything I should do, and he said I should ring Christine Beales.

Christine said it was time to reel my father in. God had cast the line. I phoned people from the prayer group and told them that it was going to happen today. Each time I repeated the words, dread turned to relief and then courage. The day progressed and I waited for the phone call from my father just as I had in Cyprus years ago. But as the sun grew weaker and the evening descended, so too did my hope. The boys went to bed, I had a bath, and the phone remained silent. I had to go out that night and I knew this was the deadline, because by the time I returned it would be too late to receive any phone call from Cyprus.

I had asked God to protect my mind, to fill my dreams with my father and not to let the enemy trample on this day. But I ended this day of hope completely defeated. I had not asked God for this specific date; I had heard the word 'tomorrow', dreamt about my father and woken up feeling that this had all been from him. Why, when having come so close to the end of the year would God allow me to fall under such a huge weight of deception? Why, after having taught me so much about the endurance of faith, would he allow me to fall with such cutting disappointment?

The following day I met with a friend and together we walked along Littlehampton seafront. I explained everything that had just happened, the deception, disappointment, and the spiritual ache that was steadily becoming too painful. I was tired of talking about it, beginning to fear that this story had all been a device of my own creation. If that was the case, then the consequences on my faith and sanity didn't bear thinking about. I had spent years of my life following God's voice and praying with people who followed the same voice. Surely we couldn't all be deceived?

My friend reminded me that God's work in me has been real and permanent. But while I can be rattled and shaken, Christ within me can never be defeated. Upon reflection, how did I know that the word 'tomorrow' coupled with my dream, was not God illustrating how he was turning my father's heart towards me? I may have been looking at my father in a dream, but perhaps God was also showing me to him. As soon as I heard these words, all the fear and disappointment that Satan had tried to plant was ripped from me.

We walked towards the harbour, where the sea cuts a walled channel into the sleeping seafront. We stepped out along the small pier that divides the beach from the cold harbour waters. Sensing that there was nowhere left to walk on this spiritual journey, we began to pray about what to do next.

The clouds formed a grey canvas, blotting out any colour. Then we noticed a tiny hint of sun catching the water on the horizon. We prayed that the ripples of God's Holy Spirit would now bring my father to me. As we gave these prayers to God, while all around was lifeless, the reflection began to move. A silver line from the horizon danced and glittered towards us.

Our prayers gathered pace. We thanked God for his love, and watched the silver path as it touched the end of the pier. It looked like it had been painted onto the skin of the water; a delicate and metallic path that we could have walked across. The elements provided a shining confirmation that God was in charge, removing every obstacle as he prepared his path before us. I have been deceived in the past, I have also misinterpreted God's voice, but his true voice has never been wrong. All God wanted me to do was believe in what he had promised.

I wrote in my journal:

> It is now the 19 December 2004, and I am waiting for God to fulfil his promise. Since beginning the book earlier this year, it had been entitled 'My Search for a Father'. With the discovery of my 2002 diary, we have taken out the 'my' and returned the title to what God intended, 'Search for a Father'. It is the statement I believe God wants the world to hear. It is his encouragement to a generation embittered by broken relationships.

Search for a father almost becomes a command, to search for the relationships that God designed us to flourish in as families. Above all it becomes a challenge, to search for a Father in God. We need to search for our heavenly Father, because in doing so he will then reveal his plan for our lives.

This has been the hardest journey of my life, waiting, praying, watching, believing and following. But I can do all things through Christ who has strengthened me. I have seen the proof of God's miracles already, lives transformed in seemingly impossible ways, and that includes my own. Whatever the outcome of this story, the Bible says that those whose hope is in God will never be put to shame.

This is now the full stop written over the journey. There is no more to say until God reveals his ending. And so the last words belong to him, they are from Habakkuk 2:3: 'But these things I plan won't happen right away. Slowly, steadily, surely, the time approaches when the vision will be fulfilled. If it seems slow, wait patiently, for it will surely take place. It will not be delayed.' (*Extract from the New Living Translation*)

25

Phone Call

I waited for my father. In my mind, I began to picture a Christmas reunion. It was Hollywood-like in its sentiment and romance, as Theo and I were reconciled around the coloured glow of the Christmas tree.

Christmas was only a couple of weeks away. Every day I waited for my father's phone call, through which, inspired by God, he would love me. I could not imagine a better ending to this story. It was the romance that I had dreamt about since my childhood. Christmas had been a time of year bereft of parents, enhanced each season by my father's absence. It is accurate to say that I had poured hope and belief into meeting my father on Christmas Day.

By the time Christmas Eve arrived such hope had become desperation. Simon and his wife Gemma joined Tim and me for the evening. None of our parents were present, for different reasons. Questions and emotions were buried in everyone as we all felt our individual separation. The expectation of meeting my father slipped away and an uncomfortable emptiness settled in its place. I could not celebrate; I tried to pray but could say nothing. On Christmas Eve 2004, there were no words left.

I went through the motions of a traditional British Christmas, stuffing the turkey, wrapping the presents, preparing everything for the following day. I tried to be excited; but my mind was fixed on the journey's end. I was expecting the best from God. Even prayer, to a certain degree, had become a series of pleas for it to happen *now*. There was a fear that if it did not then it would not happen at all. But who am I to dictate to God? I can ask, because my prayers are not fatalistic, and I am not a puppet pulled by God's strings. I have a free will that God will not violate. But God was still asking me to wait.

By midnight I could not take any more. I cried and screamed. I frightened Tim and myself by my sudden collapse into despair. Waiting for an ending had dictated the shape of my relationships, conversations and emotions. The weight of my sisters reading the book . . . Simon writing it . . . all my friends who had prayed earnestly; all this seemed to hang above my head like a noose.

By the end of Christmas Eve I feared that my entire journey had been one of total deception. Could it be that through the genuine sadness and loss of my father, I had succeeded only in bringing about my own humiliation? Had I been clothed in the spiritual armour that the Bible describes, or wrapped in the bandages of delusion? I could no longer tell any more.

Something had to break and it was Tim who witnessed my breakdown. My mind could not be strained any further. Either I was to let go of this completely or I would be crushed under the pressure. I had arrived at the end of my belief, the limits of my faith. If this story proved to be nothing more than dreams and manipulation, I didn't know how I would possibly recover, never mind encourage anybody to believe for the impossible again.

Christmas Day became a difficult occasion to endure, affecting everyone present. The following day I took a walk along the beach. Spiritually, I could 'see' the edge of the chasm. The bridge was closed, and perhaps it always had been. All I could hear were Satan's taunts and accusations. There would be no reunion. I had made a huge mistake. It was now time to turn back. It was the sane thing to do.

I met my church pastor and we walked together. He knew the situation; lots of my friends did. They knew how I was feeling and they were supportive. But I didn't want anybody to have to walk another step with me; I wanted to let go and turn away. In the crisp December chill on a wintry Littlehampton beach, I explained to the pastor, David, that I had believed in specific words, convinced that I would meet my father either this year or while I was still thirty-two. But now I no longer knew whether I had ever heard from God.

I have spoken already about the walls of Jericho. How God told Joshua, a military man, to march his army around the city walls. The priests blew their trumpets, and on the seventh day, following an almighty battle cry, God toppled the walls for the army to take the city. God had a plan. As strange as it may have sounded to an army of soldiers, it was the strategy that God had chosen for their victory.

On the fourth day of Christmas, the clouds of confusion suddenly dispersed. When I woke up it had become clear to me what I needed to do. I would make an appointment with one of my Cypriot contacts to meet them in Cyprus and 'take the city'. It was a strategy, but was it of God? I believed that it was; it was as shining as the silver path that I had seen from the harbour.

I thought of the story of Moses. After delivering the Hebrews from centuries of Egyptian slavery, the nomadic nation of Israel was caught between the sea and Pharaoh's murderous army. On God's order Moses struck the ground with his staff and God parted the waves. Although he had been given a path of safety, Moses still had to physically walk along the divine pathway. A further act of faith was required.

I had recently been reminded of the biblical principle that faith without deed is dead. This had been hard to hear because I had not spent the last six years doing nothing. But I was angry that nothing was happening, and so further action was required. As I prepared to make the necessary phone calls to Cyprus, I had to trust that God would reveal the way forwards and give me hope.

That same day, my sister Lynn was due to visit. Anticipating her arrival, I decided to make my phone calls in the morning. The initial plan was to phone my aunt in Cyprus, tell her that I was coming to the island, and request that she first ask Theo to meet me. I phoned her number a few times, but I could not get through. Then I remembered that the number belonged to her holiday home. I phoned International Directory Enquiries. There was another number matching her name, but it was ex-directory. At this moment in time, she could not be reached.

There was one remaining number scribbled on my notepaper. It was the number that I had been told in a dream was 'the right one'. Months ago I had tried to ring it but it had not existed. I rang it. A woman answered!

With nothing to lose, I began to speak. 'I'm sorry to trouble you, but I am looking for Theodoros Antonios Selios. Does he live there?'

'Yes,' came the reply. 'He does live here.'

Astonished that the number now existed when before it hadn't, I explained that I was looking for relatives and I had been told that Theo could help me. The woman requested that I phoned back at six in the evening when he would be home. In Greece they were two hours ahead of the UK, which meant I should ring back at four o'clock. Lynn was arriving at midday; what would I tell her?

I knew that Lynn was possibly worried about me battling with this journey. She was too afraid to look at my faith, and so she only knew a small part of the story. When she arrived, I explained the day's events. Seven months ago the same phone number had not existed, now it did. A man lived there who had the name I had been looking for.

'You're not still on that one, are you?' said my sister.

'Yes,' I admitted, feeling slightly defeated.

'Mand, I don't mean to be harsh,' said Lynn, 'but I worry about you because I know what Greek men are like.'

All I could say in reply was that I was not putting my trust in man, but in God. In Lynn's opinion, this was the mindset that was prolonging my pain.

As the hour approached to ring Cyprus again, I decided to make the call without telling Lynn. Tim sat with me in the bedroom and prayed as I rang the number. This time a man answered. I asked him if his name was Theodoros Antonios Selios, and he said, 'Yes.' When I told him my own name he had difficulty pronouncing it, as though he had heard it for the first time. My heart sank because if this was my father who had read either of my letters, then he was already familiar with my name. I asked how old he was, and he said forty-four, which again didn't fit. That would have made him around twelve years old when he had met my mum at the party! I explained that I was looking for my father and asked whether he knew of any other men by the same name in his village.

He said, 'No.'

Apart from his name, which I still believed to be right, everything else about the conversation was wrong. But if this was the man who Lynn's uncle Paul had named as being my father, then even that name was now held in question. To add to the confusion, he asked me whether I had ever considered coming to Cyprus to find my father. I put the phone down and looked at Tim. I had found Theodoros Antonios Selios. The name existed. The man existed. Even if this was my father admitting to his name, he had lied about his age.

Where was the evidence that God had turned my father's heart towards me? Wasn't God supposed to have been speaking to my father all this time? Had I not prayed that it was so? Had I not written that it was so? Stunned and helpless, I had to face Lynn again. She didn't know about the second phone call, and so I chose not to tell her about it. At a time such as this I feared seeing 'I told you so' written on her face. How could I pretend that everything was fine?

I began by making the tea, hiding behind a familiar routine, but my head was spinning. I could hardly string a sentence together. Everything that had been written since January 2004, based on words of prophecy, was slowly unravelling and falling apart.

The fact that I had chosen not to tell Lynn about this conversation made the situation worse. I wanted the protection of my older sisters, and it pained me to repeatedly come against their opinions. Talking to Lynn was a battle because she didn't agree with what I was doing. But I had not been running after my father to spite my sisters. I had not placed a man who I had never met over my sisters who I knew and loved. It was because of God that I had been inspired to fight against everything that had defined my family – every single lie that hid us away in shame and told us we were nothing.

26

River Crossing

I may have been regarded by some as the young and foolish sister, but I benefited from the encouragement of friends. They asked me whether or not the Theo I had spoken to had told the truth. How did I know for certain that there wasn't another Theo? I was reminded that this was the Greek Cypriot culture I was dealing with. But that was not a reason to fear, not a reason to back down. In the eyes of God there was absolutely no honour in lying, but perhaps people had lied to honour and protect their families.

There were now more questions than answers as a result of the phone call, and so I decided to ring again the following day. Because of my first trip to Cyprus and the following chain of events, I knew that there was a man called Theo who came from the village of Ayios Theodoros. He was married when I was born, and the people who knew him had pointed out the family resemblance between us. I had seen his brother outside a Cypriot café. And I had been told what a lovely man my father was by his sister-in-law, who later advised me to pretend he was dead. Could there really be another man, living locally, who went by the same name of

Theodoros Antonios Selios? It seemed as ridiculous and unlikely as marching and blowing trumpets to besiege a city.

The following day I called the number at six in the evening, knowing that Theo would be in. Despite his heavily broken English, there was a notable softening in his tone. I told him that I had some questions for him and said, 'Do you mind me asking them?' He was accommodating, welcoming the direction of the conversation. I could only wonder, was I talking to my father? Had God turned his heart towards me? Was that happening as this very conversation took place?

I asked Theo whether he knew Capros (this was the name of my uncle). Possibly surprised that I was more familiar with his family than he expected, he said, 'Yes.' I then asked whether Capros had a brother called Theo. Again he said, 'Yes.' He had confirmed what I already knew, but it was further evidence that the name was right. If this man was not my father, then there had to be another Theo. I stepped into the heart of God's strategy. 'I am coming to Cyprus in a couple of weeks,' I said, firmly. 'When I arrive, will you meet me?'

Amazingly he said, 'Yes.'

Before the conversation ended, I told him, 'Look, I'm not mad. I've been told for years that my father's name is Theodoros Antonios Selios. I've also been told that I look like him. And even if it's simply to eliminate your name from my search, I have to meet you.'

I asked him whether he understood the meaning of the word 'eliminate', and he said he did. Without wanting to bully him, I wanted him to understand that I was serious. I closed by declaring, 'I am not the sort of person who will accept a lie; I need to find the truth.'

I put the phone down. If I had just spoken to my father, then he had just agreed to meet me in Cyprus. Perhaps he was still too afraid to admit to who he was. Perhaps he wanted to meet me first. Maybe then we would connect in some way. Whoever he was, we were destined to meet.

At the beginning of 2005, the theme of crossing the River Jordan was preached at church. This had been the challenge for Joshua who was leading the Israelites following the death of Moses, his predecessor. Moses had led over a million Israelite people through the desert. A short journey became a forty-year stretch as they repeatedly complained and disobeyed God. But the land God had promised to them was still waiting. God encouraged his church with the same words he gave to Joshua thousands of years ago.

> Be strong and courageous, because you will lead these people to inherit the land I swore to their forefathers to give them . . . Be careful to obey all the law my servant Moses gave you; do not turn from it to the right or to the left, that you may be successful wherever you go. Do not let this Book of the Law depart from your mouth; meditate on it day and night, so that you may be careful to do everything written in it. Then you will be prosperous and successful. (Josh. 1:6–8)

To reach the occupied land that God had set aside for the nation of Israel, they first had to cross the River Jordan.

Inspired by this timely message to take the Promised Land, I placed my sights on Cyprus. I booked a flight for 14 January 2005. This time Tim would accompany me. As husband and wife, we set out to claim a father and a father-in-law.

On the plane to Cyprus I distracted myself by watching the in-flight movie. I could only pray that this time I would not be travelling back without first seeing my father. When we landed, we jumped in a taxi and arrived at a hotel. We decided to stay in the same hotel that Christine Beales and I had occupied during my first trip. It was called The Athens, but through my muddled Greek pronunciation I had mistakenly pronounced it 'Athenie'. We booked in for a four-day visit, and at six o'clock I phoned Theo.

He greeted me with great excitement and we agreed to meet at the hotel at eight. When he asked where I was, I said, 'The Athenie,' and he said, 'Where's that?'

Once again my expectation was dealt another blow. My father would have known the hotel because he once worked there. I gave Theo brief directions that were probably a little too general, and we agreed that he would ring me from the hotel foyer. When he asked my full name he struggled to pronounce 'Lord'. Between my poor directions and our mutual fumbling over each other's languages, it would take a miracle for us to meet at all. I asked Tim to pray that Theo would find his way to us. My heart was a lead weight. I was convinced that this man was not my father. If not, then what was God's plan for this meeting?

I prepared myself in a typically girly way, checking my hair and wondering whether my clothes were right. I asked Tim how I looked and he said, 'Fine.' It was not the most tactful of answers. During this time, I made a final and frantic attempt to figure out the nature of this meeting. Perhaps Theo was a brother or cousin, who upon seeing the family resemblance would talk to my father with an inspired perspective. As I waited in the hotel room to meet a stranger, all that I could do was give this dream back to God. It was his vision.

At twenty minutes to eight the phone rang in our hotel room. I picked it up and a lady from reception apologised for disturbing us. She said that there were two men waiting for me in the hotel lobby.

'There are two men, Tim! Two!' I panicked. 'Do you think that one of them could be my dad?'

Tim met my eyes with his usual patience, encouraging me to remain calm. We left the room and took the lift to the hotel reception. The doors opened and I saw two Greek men sitting in the lobby. When they saw Tim and me they rose to their feet.

It took a couple of seconds for us all to look at one another. In that moment, six years of faith and desperation and a lifetime of dreams were channelled into searching the two strangers for a glimmer of recognition. The meeting burned its imprint on my memory. I asked which of the two men had spoken to me on the phone. The younger and darker skinned man stepped forwards. As I was able to match the name and voice to this man, I knew in that instant that *this* Theodoros Antonios Selios was not my father.

He introduced himself.

'I am Antonios, and this is Theo.' He gestured towards the older man standing by his side; he was very Mediterranean in appearance and distinguished in his features. I looked at the two men, overwhelmed by the meeting, and now confused by their names. They invited us to the café next door and Tim and I left the hotel with them. They ordered drinks and we all sat down together.

I looked at Tim and whispered, 'That's my dad!' referring to Antonios's older guest.

Again Tim was cautious. 'Hang on,' he said, 'let's just hear what they have to say.'

The café was very ordinary, and we sat around a rectangular coffee table. The way we were seated placed me furthest away from our mysterious guest, Theo. The younger man apparently preferred to be called Antonios. He said very little, but the older man became very animated. He placed his hand on his heart and announced, 'I am so happy to meet you.' He said that I was pretty and then the two men spoke in Greek, hopefully agreeing on the matter! I had tried to look my best. Then he gestured again, and repeated, 'I am so happy to meet you.'

While my heart thumped against my chest, I thought, *Why are you happy to meet me? Who are you? Are you really my father?*

As though he had heard my silent question, the distinguished man looked across the table and explained, 'It is because of your persistence that I am here right now.' He said it again and began to cry. 'I am so ashamed!' he wept. 'I am so ashamed. How could I put you through all of this?'

Then Antonios began to cry, and so did Tim as he tapped me on the leg and said gently, 'This is your dad. Go and hug him.'

I walked around the table, pulled up a chair next to Theo, sat down and hugged him. I could feel the Holy Spirit at work as I sensed a deep connection between this man and myself. It was like a spiritual light turning on, the way Tim had described his own feelings of fatherhood when he first saw Ethan. But after seven years of endless lies and doubts I needed confirmation.

I asked this stranger, 'Are you my dad?

In his heavy Greek accent he said, 'Yes. I am your dad.'

As I hugged my father, we all cried. It was all we could do.

If that moment was not amazing enough, my father's next words defied all expectation. 'This is of God! This is of God!' he repeated excitedly, caught in the emotion of the reunion. I pulled away from him and looked at his face.

'You are so beautiful,' I told him, and held his face in both my hands. God was unleashing his love, and I wanted my father to receive all the love that had driven me to find him. I wiped away one of his tears with my thumb and said, 'I know this is of God. Your name is Theo. It means "Gift from God". You are a gift from God.'

We sat frozen in this moment for about fifteen minutes, but it felt like fifteen seconds. I drank a glass of white wine; I remember the taste but not drinking it. I remember crying, then talking, then crying again. I remember my dad's face and his tears. There were so many tears of joy as thirty-two years of spiritual yearning were condensed into this intense and unique embrace.

Theodoros Antonios Selios was my father. He was also my cousin, as both men shared the same name! Antonios was just as emotional as my father, his uncle. He was a published poet, and told my father that the moment was so beautiful he already had a poem in mind. And as for the confusion about the name – when he'd told me on the phone that he didn't know anyone else by that name – well, maybe I'll never know why that was said.

Tim took a handful of photographs and began to text people back home. Everybody would want to know what God had done. Tim and I had been prepared for a long haul and a ferocious spiritual battle of prayer and persistence. Now that battle was over and Tim's face was shining too. He looked bathed in happiness; released from the years of pain he had seen me go through. Our lives may have suddenly changed forever, but around that table the presence of God was the same as yesterday, today and tomorrow.

Dreams change. People change. The world changes around us. But God is unchanging. He is the one thing we can rely on. Six years ago he promised that I would meet my father. At the end of 2003 he told Simon it would happen while I was thirty-two years old and that this relationship was eternal in its design. I had only known my father for twenty minutes, but I felt like I had known him all my life. Tim noted that it was as though he had brought me up. When I hugged Theo I felt the Holy Spirit as real as a fifth person at the coffee table. My father said with conviction, 'I took one look at you and all the darkness left me.'

The Fireguard

Picture a fire on a cold winter's day
Feel the warmth that it gives
As the ice melts away.
See the leap of its flames
With the temperature rising
As it dances its call to you
Light, mesmerising.
Drawing you close to its warming surround
Such tempting a welcome not easily found.
You would think it was safe
It would never do harm
But its glow, a façade, for such deadly a charm.
The life that it offers bears so great a cost
The more that you share with it, the more you have
    lost.
For it burns us with lies that it's safe – there's no
    fear
And consumes all that foolishly stray closer than near.
Like an army of locusts devour all in their way
Or a lion on the prowl its victim to slay.
There's no end to its fury, the burning within
Like a heart full of hatred, a life lost in sin.

So guard yourself from its touch, don't fuel the fire
Don't fall to temptation, resist the desire.

When the fuel of temptation is found in your way
The fire of sin, that leads us astray,
There's a face you can turn to
A fortress, a helper.
A guard from the flames, a healer, a shelter.
In his guard you are safe
From the flames that surround,

No scars from the burns
But life and new ground.

27

Dancing Father

There were few communication barriers between my father and me. He spoke better English than my cousin Antonios. They wanted to take us to a restaurant with real Greek food and music. While Tim spoke to Antonios, I walked arm in arm with my father. We were joined together in victory as father and daughter, parent and child. I told him that I knew we would be so alike, and we were. Everything I was feeling he was speaking out. For every time I thought, *Thank you God*, my father spoke it into the warm and inviting evening air of Larnaca. When I stopped to reflect on how beautiful he was, he would tell me how beautiful I was to him. He put into words the beatings of my heart.

Tim contacted people in England, telling everyone how he was about to have dinner with his father-in-law. His phone did not stop ringing with the voices of our stunned friends. In the restaurant I made sure that I sat next to Theo. I looked at Tim to make sure he was fine. The expression of amazement never once left his face. Theo touched very little on his plate, and I had just enough to soak up the wine! It was just so wonderful sitting in a Greek restaurant with my dad. I had dreamt of this since sitting in such a restaurant as a teenager, convinced that Mum was about to tell me about my father. The early days of the search took me to Nicky's restaurant and took Tim to Paul's on the offensive. But now I was here at the end, and it was so perfect. What I had longed for over Christmas had been a shallow undercoat of the vibrancy and colour of this reunion.

Theo looked at me and announced without embarrassment, 'Right, I am going to dance for you now.' He rose from the table and danced without shame to the staccato rhythm of the traditional Greek music. As the restaurant looked on, I felt God say, 'You have danced for your father for so long, now it is time for him to dance for you.'

I had to pinch myself. God had turned my father's heart towards me in a reunion beyond anything I had been capable of dreaming of. Theo called me over and we danced together. I don't think that I have ever smiled so much in my life. When we finally sat down again to join Tim and Antonios, Theo grabbed Tim's arm in excitement. 'You might think that I am crazy, but you know what, God can actually speak to you.'

Of course Tim knew this, but we had not yet breathed a word to Theo about our faith. As he instigated the conversation, Tim and I looked at each other in disbelief. My father had danced for me. Now he was expressing his faith in the Father who had brought us both together. Theo spoke again, choosing his words carefully, 'God told me about a year ago that one day a book of my life would be written.'

Tim was stunned and said, 'Amanda! You tell him.'

'Back in my hotel room,' I explained, 'I have a book and it's called *Search for a Father*. It's about you. We have come to Cyprus to find the last chapter of the book, and it is you. You are the last chapter.'

Now Theo sat in disbelief. We hugged and the celebrations began all over again. Eventually it was time to leave the restaurant behind. Theo insisted on paying the bill, and because our celebrations had been noticed, he explained to the staff that I was his daughter and we had just met for the first time. There was a buzz of excitement surrounding our reunion. It was the kind of story that touched a cultural nerve in the Cypriot heart. The restoration of a relationship believed lost touches a deep spiritual nerve the world over. It is the reality that Jesus has offered us, evident in the millions of people who are restored back to God through his sacrifice.

My father had lived a life separated from me by guilt. Now God released him to be a father to his lost daughter. I was no longer a daughter of shame. No longer hidden. God had broken my father's fear and denial of our relationship. God had planned this long ago because he delights in the restoration of family. In accepting the resurrected life of Jesus, I had been brought back to my heavenly Father. It was only because of him that I was able to sit with my earthly father after thirty-two years of separation and pain.

We walked back to the hotel, exposed and protected by God's love. As we hugged for the last time that night, Theo declared that his heart was breaking already. It was a reflection of God's heart, breaking for every single person who leaves him.

Later that night I spoke to my friends on the phone. They all cried and laughed with me. There would be many more reactions. Those who had prayed for this reunion now knew that every single prayer had reached the throne of God. Every single tear had been counted and wiped away. Every test of faith and every human doubt had been worth the pain. God had kept his promise.

On the second morning of our stay in Cyprus, I found myself desperate to speak to my friend Christine Beales.

'Christine, you'll never believe what has just happened,' I said on the phone.

'What? Tell me, tell me!' she cried.

'I've just met my dad! And it was more than I had ever dreamed it would be.'

'What did he look like?' Christine asked.

'He's lovely and I look like him. And he's already got a relationship with God . . . Oh I have to go – my dad's waiting for me downstairs.'

I laughed at what I had just said.

'I've never said that sentence before!'

The hotel lobby rang; my dad was downstairs waiting. Together we walked to the restaurant arm in arm. He led the conversation; he was very organised, taking our contact numbers. I asked him to phone my sister Lynn. I needed Lynn to know that the man I had never known had finally come through for me. We called Lynn. I said, 'Lynn, there's someone here who wants to speak to you.' She was a bit shocked, but also happy for me.

My dad physically shook as he spoke to my sister; it was very emotional for him. He told her about how sorry he was, which took the pressure off me to have to convince her that the relationship and its future was genuine. Theo was genuine, and Lynn could tell by talking to him that he was a good man.

It was Saturday morning and we shared breakfast. Once again, I could hardly touch my food. My stomach was still churning from the nervous excitement of the occasion. We arranged that my dad would see us on the Monday morning, the day we were due to leave. He was working from three in the afternoon until eleven in the evening for a local insurance firm, and apart from working the weekends he also wanted to spend the Sunday morning with his wife. After our meeting, my dad went to work and Tim and I returned to the hotel to get some more sleep. I woke up again at five in the afternoon. The phone rang. It was Theo asking to meet us again that night after work, as he could not wait until Monday.

We walked along Larnaca beach together. It was the same beach that I had walked with Christine Beales on my previous visit to Cyprus. Then I had cried to God about why I was going home without having met him, frustrated at the seeming injustice of it all, wondering why I had ever come in the first place. Theo put his arm around my shoulders, and we talked about the future, about when he would tell his wife and that God had it under control, just as he had when I had first walked along the Cypriot sand. I told Theo of all the events in my life that God had spoken to me about before they had happened.

On the Sunday morning I attended a church with Tim. This was the same church that Christine and I had attended before. The service was about the crossing of the River Jordan to enter the Promised Land. It was a quiet, orderly service, and it was great to sit in God's presence again.

God made everything perfect. I needed time to absorb all that was happening, to calm down and take it all in as best I could. Emotionally, it was very intense, and it was good for Tim and me to spend some time together. We made more phone calls and talked to friends back home. We visited the church of Lazarus, lit candles and prayed for Theo's family. And of course we visited another Greek restaurant. As we ate, we listened to a man singing a mixture of traditional Greek songs and songs by artists that both my mum and Tim's mum used to love: John Denver, Gene Pitney, Elvis, Roy Orbison.

We sat in silence in between times of recounting what had unravelled before us, asking ourselves what it all meant, what God's bigger picture could be. The two of us were dumbfounded at what God had just delivered into our lives. The world had changed overnight, as it had when I had prayed for God to enter it for the first time.

That evening we met with Theo again and talked about our faith: the faith it had taken to pursue him, but faith that God had given me, because without it, I would have given up long ago. In fact, it was only a month ago that both Tim and I had doubted everything, including the contents of this book. Sitting in the café next door to the hotel, as we had done the night before, Tim and I listened as my dad talked. We wanted to gently find out about his faith. Interestingly, Tim and I had noticed that not only were our personalities and mannerisms very similar, but so too was the way in which my father and I expressed our relationship with God. We talked about the events leading to our meeting. He spoke about the letters that had been brought to Cyprus years ago. He was with his mother, who had since died, when a man from the village brought the first letter to his door. We spoke about his relationship with Nicky and how Theo had felt during the different episodes of the search. I wanted to know my father's side of the story.

Being a man of God, my father told me that normally he would have prayed for direction, but my arrival in his life had thrown him into panic. He was a respected and honourable man in his home village, despite being seen as slightly crazy for his less formal and less 'religious' faith. When he discovered that he had an English daughter, he could not reconcile his respected present with his shameful past. With the arrival of the letter, and then Nicky carrying the second, and the contact with his sister-in-law, the entire village knew of the situation. He lied, saying that he had nothing to do with the accusations from England.

I could tell that Theo had encountered God, but it was becoming apparent that he had received no teaching. With only the Bible to guide him through isolation, a lot of his opinions were unrefined. He was very much still on the early part of his journey, but I could relate to that. Every Christian is on a journey with God which never stands still during this lifetime. But I had experienced the privilege of strong Christian teaching during my first steps. The Elim church had allowed God's Spirit to counsel. It had been a place where teaching and ministry were available, proving to be an invaluable spiritual backdrop to my marriage and the birth of my two sons.

It was never in my heart to bully or interrogate my father. God had made me wait for this time, and I simply wanted to know him. Despite never having known him, I had always loved him, and so forgiving my father for the lies and the deceit was not an issue.

Monday arrived. It was a morning that held a bitter-sweet taste. In a few hours' time I would be on the plane home. Shattered after another restless night, we prepared to meet my dad for breakfast again. I wanted to buy him a present. We went out shopping and returned with the perfect gift; a gold-plated pen that sat in a distinguished presentation case. As soon as I saw it I was reminded of what we were fighting to achieve with our faith, the writing of the book, the declaration so long ago that all this would take place. It reminded me of the picture that Tim's brother Simon had once seen of a pen and its case. It served as another connection, another stitch in the tapestry. At this point, my dad told me that he had lied to my aunt about being my father; he contacted my aunt right then and tearfully told her the truth – and I was able to speak with her and really rejoice with her (it also turned out that the mix-up with the number of the record shop – another setback – had been a genuine mistake).

Meeting my dad was seeing the physical result of so many connecting prayers: prayers that had been emotional, quiet and reflective, desperate and dry, enthused and passionate. It had begun as a belief that God told me I would meet my dad one day. The belief had become a prayer, prayed through repeatedly as the wait and the pain was lived out in reality. And now I was witnessing God's answer to every single one of those prayers.

One of the members of our youth group had once prayed for me that meeting my dad would be like wearing a crown. And that it would be time to put my head up, my shoulders back, and wear that crown. Growing up in England, I viewed every Greek-looking man with the eyes of a lost daughter. When I had first ventured to Cyprus my head was bowed. Not only because I was surrounded by elderly Greek men, but also because I was ashamed. I had grown to apologise for my existence and the circumstances that had caused it. That cloud of shame followed me into my Christian walk, and I was embarrassed at who I was and my failings in the light of who I wanted to be.

We met my dad again. He did not miss an opportunity to introduce me to everyone that he knew, friends and acquaintances; wherever we went he told people that I was his daughter. My posture changed and for the first time in my life I felt proud to be someone's daughter.

Theo took me to a jeweller. I felt like a princess. He told the woman behind the counter who I was and then he bought me a ring. It was a gift from my father, as he himself had been a gift from my Father above.

What a delightful privilege to know God. It had not only taken six years for this meeting to happen, but also for God to convince me that when it happened, it would be a good thing. His gift would become something to celebrate and not fear. And he did have to convince me. Over the years I had experienced many doubts, one of them being whether I would meet my dad once, only for him to fade into obscurity again. God has had to reassure me since my previous empty-handed visit to Cyprus, that when I met my dad it would be a good relationship. It would not become a secret, but a living relationship that would bless my life and the life of my family. At times, being with my father was completely overwhelming. It was similar to when I met Tim. Despite the struggles of that early relationship, I knew that it had been under God's direction, and therefore it was good. God longs to bring reconciliation between people, and ultimately between people and himself. It brought great freedom knowing that he was in control. It allowed me to become vulnerable; I could tell my dad that I loved him without the fear of him leaving again.

People have asked me how I could love my father for all the years he remained nothing but a dream. I can never explain why; it was just something that I was able to do. In hindsight, I consider it one of God's many gifts that even as a little girl, damaged by the world, I was unable to build walls around my heart when it came to loving my father.

There are such huge walls that can be built around our hearts, but the good news is that they always have a breaking point. That is why we need to pray for God to turn the hearts of the fathers towards their children, and vice versa, because he will. Jesus knocks on the door to our hearts all our lives, and when he is invited in, he becomes our protector. Our homemade defences are no

longer needed. In loving my dad I have experienced
God's heart for the fatherless, which is why I cannot
agree with people who say they don't need a father, or
who diminish the role of the father, because God is a
father and he shares his father's love with us.

28

Theodoros Antonios Selios

Having returned home and shared the news with my friends, family and church, life settled down. But now I had a father who I could speak to on the phone as often as I liked – and a relationship to build. I had thought for a long time that my father's voice should be present at the end of this story. So with the help of a Dictaphone and a telephone, I asked my dad to share something from his perspective. This was his explanation – in his own words:

> One day I was sitting on the veranda at my mother's house, a few years before she died. My cousin, Anthony Selios, handed me a letter that he had brought from the village post office. He did not say a word; he looked very serious and he left immediately. I knew that it was not an ordinary letter; it contained some very special and serious news.
>
> I opened it and without hiding my pain from my mother, I began to read. I was astonished and shocked. It was Amanda saying to me that she was my daughter and that she had been searching for me for many years. She had found me through a friend in England who was

also from the village of Ayios Theodoros. Thirty-three years ago, this friend had taken me to Amanda's mother's party in Eastbourne, and so it happened that we spent the night together.

My mother asked me what was written in the letter. I replied with a pretend smile that it was just an ordinary letter and nothing to worry about. When I left the village to return to my home in the town of Larnaca, I could not stop thinking about the letter. I knew without a doubt that Amanda was my daughter because I could remember every single detail about that evening in Eastbourne. I did not think that her mother could be pregnant, as she told me that she was taking the pill. I was even invited back to visit, but I never did.

About Nicky, I heard that he had contacted my brother. He was asking for my number because he wanted to speak to me. I found out that a girl from England wanted to find me. I was surprised. Nicky kept calling my brother asking the same questions. But I said that I knew nothing about it. As far as I was concerned I did not have a daughter in England.

When John [*the taxi driver*] phoned my house, I was away. My wife answered, and when I returned home she said that somebody from the village wanted to speak to me. After a little while he phoned again and I answered. My wife was standing next to me and so I pretended that I was speaking to a customer about car insurance. On the other end of the phone, John explained to me very clearly that Amanda had come to Cyprus especially to meet me.

Of course, I knew about her by now, but I did not know what to do. John insisted that I should meet with this English girl, and so I agreed, but I explained to him my concerns about people asking what I was doing and why. A lot of people knew about the situation. A lot of people had told me about how I had a daughter in

England. This was because Nicky had told them. In the end I decided not to go to the hotel. I knew that I was not doing the right thing, but I was so scared that my wife and children would find out.

I had not spoken to my sister-in-law [*Amanda's aunt, who was called Kay*] very much, but one day I decided to ring her. She said that she had wanted to talk to me about something, but was not sure what to do. A girl kept phoning, claiming to be my daughter.

I knew all about it, but I told Kay that I knew nothing and could not understand why somebody would make that claim.

Kay tried to persuade me to speak with Amanda, because she wanted to help. She said that Amanda had sounded desperate to meet me. But I insisted that I knew nothing about it. I did not tell Kay that Amanda was my daughter, and so when she made that same statement to Amanda, it was not because she was lying, but because I had lied. I knew the importance of the situation, it was very serious, but I wondered why, after so many years, Amanda wanted to meet me. Was her intention to hurt either my family or me? It was then that I told myself that if Amanda was genuine and I really was her father, then I would wait. God would help me to find a solution. God had to help me because I did not know what to do.

My nephew Anthony [*Antonios*] told me that he had spoken to Amanda on the phone. He desperately wanted me to meet her. When I heard this I at last said yes. Anthony told me that Amanda was very sensitive and that I could not be cruel to her any more. I decided that when she phoned Anthony again, he was to agree to meet her.

I believe that God wanted us to meet. I knew that Amanda was my daughter as soon as I read her letter, but it took years to really accept this. I believe that God had to keep reminding me, and to keep telling Amanda to persist in wanting to meet me.

My nephew Anthony phoned again, having arranged a time to meet Amanda. The hotel name he gave me was wrong, but we guessed that by The Athenie, Amanda actually meant The Athens. With some detective work and the help of the local taxi drivers, we were able to find the right hotel. When we arrived at the hotel reception we realised that not only had the hotel name been confused on Amanda's part but so too was Amanda's surname on our part. We tried asking for Lyude and Lyoot, but not Lord. The man at the reception desk showed us the customer list on the computer, until the manageress shouted at him. She did not want to help us and thought that we were up to no good, possibly involving customers and drugs. And so we decided to leave because we could not find the right name. As we were about to leave I was filled with courage and determination that I believe came from God, and I said to the lady, 'Will you please have a look for a name similar to Lyoot?'

She found the name Lord. I asked her to ring the room and Amanda answered.

I remember waiting with Anthony.

When Amanda emerged from the lift, the look in her face told me that she was my daughter. After we all greeted one another, we sat in the café next door. Amanda sat in front of me, and we both looked at each other. I told her that she was my daughter because she looked like me and I felt this stronger than ever. Then I realised how much she had suffered for me and I cried. She hugged me and said that I was her father.

Amanda was in my heart. My heart was burning for my daughter.

My father's words have brought healing to me. And he continues to send kind, encouraging messages. But our most recent milestone has been taking a DNA test, so that others could see some clinical proof that we are father and daughter.

We went to this vast building with a marble floor. It was very posh. My dad kept telling the staff about our story. And they listened intently as he explained how we had found each other.

Now I have in my possession an official document from the Cyprus Institute of Neurology and Genetics. The test results confirm that Theodoros is my dad. I thought I knew God as my father – and to some extent I did. But he has allowed me to find my knight in shining armour.

Miracle Maker

I'm waiting here
For my life to change.
When the waters stir
You can rearrange me
Just one touch, is all I need.
I've nothing much
But the wounds I feel.
I'm looking for the hands
Of the miracle man.

Holy, you are Holy,
Who was and is, and is to come.
Holy, you are Holy, Saviour, Healer.
I'm standing at the feet
Of the miracle maker.

I'm holding on
With your life in mine.
Living water come
And you've rearranged me.

Holy, you are Holy,
Who was and is, and is to come.
Holy, you are Holy, Saviour, Healer.
I'm staring in the face
Of the miracle maker.

Holy, you are Holy,
Who was and is, and is to come.
Holy, you are Holy, Saviour, Healer.
I'm walking in the shoes
Of my miracle maker.

I'm standing with the faith
Of a miracle maker.

Smith/Garrard/Thatcher/Smith/Jupp
© 2005 *Curious? Music UK*

Here is a song written by a member of the youth group just after I met my dad for the first time.

When all else starts to fade
And all I feel is pain
Your hope is all I have
Will your hand guide my way?

You have heard my cry
Searching for my Saviour
Turn your heart to me
Your love makes me complete
Bring hope to the fatherless
Strength to the weak

For I will one day meet you
Your promise is true
My soul delights
The father in you

Lead me, take me
Don't forsake me
Hold me in your arms
I'm desperate for a glimpse of what I'm looking, fighting for
No more hurt, no more pain
I find peace in your rain

Tom Smith © 2006